T0354576

HOME IS WHERE THE HEART IS

A Memoir

BRYCE ROBERTSON

WESTBOW
PRESS®
A DIVISION OF THOMAS NELSON
& ZONDERVAN

WestBow Press books may be ordered through booksellers or by contacting:

WestBow Press
A Division of Thomas Nelson & Zondervan
1663 Liberty Drive
Bloomington, IN 47403
www.westbowpress.com
1 (866) 928-1240

Because of the dynamic nature of the Internet, any web addresses or
links contained in this book may have changed since publication and
may no longer be valid. The views expressed in this work are solely those
of the author and do not necessarily reflect the views of the publisher,
and the publisher hereby disclaims any responsibility for them.

Any people depicted in stock imagery provided by Getty Images are
models, and such images are being used for illustrative purposes only.
Certain stock imagery © Getty Images.

ISBN: 978-1-9736-3658-8 (sc)
ISBN: 978-1-9736-3659-5 (hc)
ISBN: 978-1-9736-3657-1 (e)

Library of Congress Control Number: 2018910188

Print information available on the last page.

WestBow Press rev. date: 09/25/2018

Contents

Introduction

The Reverend Allison Jean from St. Andrew United Methodist Church in Plano, Texas, was the preacher for chapel at Highland Springs one day. In the delivery of her sermon, she commented that many of us were "living in Lent when we should be living in Easter." (Permission was given to use her phrase.)

After much reflection, I began to think that her assessment was right on target. As I was preparing to release the manuscript of my memoirs to the publishers, I realized how relevant her statement was to the text I was about to have put into print.

As I have reexamined my life, I realized that for my first twenty-two years, I was desperately in search of something that only God could give me. I tried but could not achieve it on my own. I wanted to be good and to experience the better life, but I realized that it could not be earned; it could only be received. It took the Holy Scriptures and a kindly old preacher to make me aware of it. So what I hope to portray in this book is that the Lenten part of my life simply was the prelude that allowed God to open the door for me to invite Easter to enter into my life in a glorious way.

My mantra is as stated: "One cannot change the beginning; but one can start where he is and change the ending."

I had a very deprived upbringing. We lived in substandard housing all of my early life. We always had food on the table, but it was not the most nourishing or healthy. We were not "poor trash," but "they lived next door."

When I left home at eighteen years of age, I made a promise to my mother that when I came home from the navy, I would be a changed person, and thanks be to God, I came home ready and willing to have my life transformed. Through the miracle of grace, God made it happen.

CHAPTER 1

Prelude to Ministry

In 1951, I was serving in the US Navy aboard the cruiser USS *Helena* off the east coast of North Korea. We were near Wonsan Harbor and attempting to eliminate the shore batteries up and down North Korea as well as to destroy mines the North Koreans had generously dumped into the waters surrounding their country.

For some time, we had been anticipating that we would soon be relieved, which would allow us to return to the States. So we were making plans for our return home.

I was a member of a committee that decided to do something special for a handicapped child in the United States. We had run our plans by the ship's authority and had been given full approval to proceed. Our gift campaign went exceedingly well. We left no stone unturned, contacting every officer and enlisted man for a contribution. After about two weeks of constant fundraising, we had acquired the amazing amount of $6,500. That was a lot of money from a group of sailors, especially in 1951.

Upon full discussion of which city to pick for our fundraiser, I recommended Helena, Montana, because our ship was named after that capital. Therefore, we wrote the chamber of commerce in Helena and asked it to send us several profiles of young children who qualified as candidates for our gift. Our request was airlifted, along with the ship's mail, to Japan, where the mail was transferred to the desired destinations.

Upon receiving our orders, we were to proceed to Sasebo, Japan, to prepare for our journey homeward. By the time we had made all the preparations, we received our response from the chamber in Helena. It had sent us eight or ten profiles.

We then set sail from Sasebo to Pearl Harbor in the Hawaiian Islands. The trip usually took about nine days, traveling at about twenty knots per hour. Nine days later, we arrived there and dispatched a committee member to fly to Helena to bring the young recipient and his foster parents to Long Beach, California, to greet our ship in about five days.

Much to our surprise, awaiting our arrival in Hawaii was the governor of Montana along with the mayor of Helena and other Montana dignitaries. All embarked our ship and sailed with us to Long Beach. It was a time to become acquainted with our honored guests and to celebrate what we had accomplished in our desire to serve a worthy candidate.

When we arrived in Long Beach, a pilot vessel met us in the outer harbor to escort us to our berth at one of the city piers. As we moved toward our berth, we were again surprised, this time seeing a monstrous crowd of nearly twenty-five thousand people cheering us home and standing on the piers and tops of buildings. We could not believe it!

As we moved into our berth, we were utterly astounded when a crew of national television reporters boarded our ship to the sound of a cheering audience. My heart rose to my throat when I remembered that I had been selected by my companions to offer the presentation speech before such an august body of people.

The young boy we had chosen was eight years of age. Dressed in his new cowboy suit adorned with a hat, pistols, boots, and a kerchief, he quickly took his place, accompanied by his foster parents and many honored guests, including the largest entourage of naval officers—of various ranks—I had ever seen. They quickly assembled in a grandstand that had been set up by the crew. My heart was pounding in my chest. This was the first speech I would ever give. I kept thinking, *Pete, keep your cool. Don't do anything stupid!* To stand before national television camera crews was not simply an honor but also the most frightening moment I had ever faced, except receiving enemy fire.

After what seemed like an eternity, I finished my remarks and knelt beside the boy, with the captain on the other side, and presented him the check that had been so generously donated by the officers and men of the USS *Helena.* I could not have been prouder or more honored.

Everything was a blur after that. I do not remember sitting down, the crowd dispersing, the many people I had met, saluting anyone, or anything else. Blank! The next thing I remember was being in my compartment and packing my seabag to begin my journey home for two weeks of leave. After about two hours, I went up to the deck, hoping the guests had left, because I did not want to see anyone. I was still a little hyper and a little unsure of how well I had performed.

As I descended the gangway, I noticed a couple standing on the pier. They had familiar faces. To my amazement, they were from my hometown in Texas and had moved to Santa Ana, California, some time ago. They had heard about our story and were there to welcome the hometown hero. I went home with them and spent the night there before I started the journey home the next day.

For many years, I wondered what had happened to this young boy. Hardly a month went by without my thinking about him in some way. The boy had become a part of me. Then, after sixty-two years, I decided to get in contact with him. I pulled up the white pages telephone directory for Helena, Montana, and found his name. One Sunday afternoon, I determined to call him. I dialed the phone, my heart pounding, and it rang several times. He would now be seventy years old, but I could still see him as a boy of eight. But there was no answer.

The next Sunday, I tried again. After three or four rings, a male voice answered the phone. I asked, "Is this Perry?"

The man said, "No, I am his son. Would you like to speak to my dad?"

I said that I would. In a short moment, another voice said hello.

I said, "My name is Bryce Robertson. I do not know if you remember me, but I remember you. I am the man who handed you the check aboard the *Helena* many years ago."

He quickly said, "I remember you as if it were yesterday!"

I said, "I have always wondered what happened to you. Do you mind sharing with me something of your life?"

He began by telling me an extraordinary story. "My foster father was a banker. He took the check and invested it from the time I was eight years old until I graduated from high school. He said there was enough money in the fund to send me to college."

I responded with something like, "I am so glad that we were able to be a part of your education."

Then he said, "Mr. Robertson, you may not know that I became a minister."

"Well, you probably don't know that I also became a minister," I replied.

We exchanged our stories for a while, and then I said to him words that did not come from me but that formed in my mouth. "Perry, neither you nor I will ever know how God has worked His way in our lives. Perhaps it was through the gift we gave and you received."

These words have become indelible on my heart and mind. I genuinely believe that this was God's first call on my life!

And I thank God that this was not His last call on my life. In retrospect, sixty-two years later, I've seen how God can use us in ways beyond our anticipation and how He prepares us by our life experiences for the tasks He will ask us to perform.

My life, as set out in these pages, demonstrates how the Lord can use the commonest of clay to achieve His purposes.

CHAPTER 2

Tragic Origins

My story began years before I was born. I have chosen to begin with the birth of my grandfather and tell it forward from there. It is not a pretty story!

My paternal grandfather, Thomas H. Robertson, was born in 1818 in Kentucky. After the Civil War began, he joined the Tennessee Volunteers on April 10, 1861, in Edgewood, Tennessee, and was attached to Company C, Second Regiment. He was discharged in 1864. My grandfather's first wife, who had borne him two sons, died in Arkansas. He later married my grandmother, Martha Elizabeth Seminole Robertson, a full-blood Seminole Indian, in 1885. My grandparents had five children: four sons and one daughter. My father, born on April 2, 1891, was the youngest. Unbelievably, my grandfather was seventy-three years old when my father was born! My grandfather died eight days after my dad was born. I suppose he just couldn't take having another child at that age.

My father was to live a tragic childhood. Totally uneducated and unable to take care of her children, my grandmother farmed them out to neighbors who used the children as slave laborers. One's heart breaks for the poor, desperate woman in an age when there was no social aid; she did what she had to do. One's heart also breaks for the children who suffered from circumstances not of their own making and who had to live through it as best they could. As Dad told the story of his displacement at the age of four, his mother took him by wagon and mules several miles out into the country and left him with a stranger, an older woman he called Grandma Seah, and drove off with him running after the wagon until he became exhausted and fell. My dad told me nothing of his days with his guardian until he was old enough to begin learning a trade.

My dad developed an interest in carpentry. He rode a mule fourteen miles each way to visit a man who taught him how to cut rafters and other rudimentary tools of the trade. My dad followed the carpentry trade all of his life, mainly building single-family housing or remodeling older houses. Dad never learned the trades of plumbing, electrical work, or floor sanding. He always hired other professionals to do what he could not.

Dad was reared in Limestone County, Texas, in a small community named Farrar, twenty miles south of Groesbeck. He told me that his mother reclaimed him when he was older, particularly after he was learning a trade. She was exceedingly poor and needed support. Dad later moved to Crandall, Texas, where he met my mother. At the time of their getting to know each other, Dad worked in a drugstore.

There are many things I never learned about my father. He rarely mentioned his early life and went for years at a time without seeing his mother. The first time I saw her, I was eleven years old. There was little or no affection between them. I think my dad went by to see her just to see his stepsister and an older brother. They were the only members of his primary family whom I ever met. There was no special recognition or affectionate greeting. It was almost as if a relationship never existed. I could hardly wait for us to leave.

My mother was of a different mold. She was born in Panola County in deep East Texas to an unusually loving and devoted family on September 12, 1890. Her parents were Robert Jasper and Nancy Jane Youngblood, who birthed four sons and four daughters. They moved to Kaufman County in about 1896 and settled in the town of Crandall. My grandfather had migrated from Resaca, Georgia, the site of a famous Civil War battle. My mother told the story that my grandfather crossed the Mississippi River on his sixteenth birthday on his trip to Texas. It was in Panola County that my grandfather met and married Nancy Jane Weir. It was a marriage of two Christian people who later reared their children in the faith, and all of them remained close to God and the church all of their days. My grandmother died an early death in 1899. My mother grew up with a single parent, assisted by an aunt who was a spinster. My mother was a strong believer and did her utmost to instill into her children a love for God and His church, to which she remained faithful all of her days. I believe to this day that my mother was my "patron saint" to whom I owe enormous gratitude for the life I have come to love, in service to my risen Lord.

CHAPTER 3

Memory, One of God's Greatest Gifts

These are a series of early memories I faintly recall. The details are not clearly explained, but I have taken each one as far as I can under the limitations of age and the function of retention. I wish that I could supply more actual facts, but age and time have erased them from the glow of my childhood. I am positive that what I am writing is true, but many of the details have been washed out with time.

Earliest Memory

The earliest memory that I recall is not the date of my birth, July 10, 1930, but the day I can envision and recall in the walls of memory what was going on, which was the first time that experience recorded on my brain an event or person. Did it happen? Absolutely! Can I prove it? No. Do I need scientific evidence to show that it really happened? No. Then how do I know it really happened? I know it because I experienced it. The brain is one of the most remarkable organs God ever created. The brain has eyes of its own, with some kind of internal mechanism that can recall what one cannot prove, yet it records events and situations and preserves them for an indefinite period of time. Memory is like a photograph that fades with time until the images can no longer be seen or remembered. Memory is not hallucination. The first is based on fact, the other on perception and imagination.

I must have been about three years old. In my mind's eye, I can see my mother, probably in the kitchen and likely facing the cabinet that was against the back wall of the kitchen. I can see the inside of the house in which we lived. The only furniture I can see is a straight chair, like an old dining room chair, turned over, with the top of the chair and the front edge resting on the floor, and I was pushing the chair as if it were a plow, with my hands resting on the back two legs of the upturned chair. I was somehow mimicking my father with his hands on the handles of a Georgia stock, an early American plow.

Since I had no other toy, the chair occupied endless hours of my time as I was, no doubt, engaged in assisting my father in the tilling of the ground and the planting of the crops. In my mind's eye, I did this day after day and with great pleasure.

Faint Memory Enforced by Mother's Retelling

I do remember faintly the small country church where my family worshipped. I remember my mother telling me that, as a small boy, I did sing occasionally during worship, to her and the congregation's pleasure. Today, and as I was growing up, I cannot imagine doing as well as my mother thought I did. But who am I to say? My mother was a living saint to me.

Clear Memory—About Four Years Old

As the first step in the separation of our family, my older brother, Wayne, had earlier found a bride in one Gertrude McCormack and chose to stay behind near Gertrude's family. I remember a time when Wayne had come to get me in order for me to spend the night with him and Gertrude, who lived about two miles from my parents. I was very excited because it my first night to spend away from my parents.

When nighttime came, I was forced to sleep between Wayne and Gertrude because they had only one bed, but I was excited and felt safe being away from my parents. However, there was a slight complication—my brother was suffering from an itch. He was forced to get up every two hours to administer a compound to his body that consisted of a mixture of sulfur and kerosene, I think, or something that was repugnant to my nose. But something else was terribly wrong: I was feeling homesick and longed to be with my parents. To my surprise, and with great joy, my father came for me that next morning, announcing that my mother had baked me a cake. I could not wait to go home. It was my first feeling that "home is where the heart is."

Memory of Early Education

My most beloved friend when I was around the age of four was my sister, Frankie. She was about two and a half years older than me, and she began her first year in school in what must have been 1934. One of the earliest experiences in my life was that she homeschooled me her first two years in public school. Frankie would come home every day after school and teach me what she had learned that day. I always looked forward to it.

It was Frankie who instilled in me the joy of learning. I will forever be grateful to her for being the one who introduced me to books and learning in the early disciplines. Because of her, I was to expand my knowledge, which led me into a career that is priceless. There is something exciting about beginnings. People can go wherever their interests lead them and enjoy the journey immensely. Had I not become interested in learning and exploring the options for my life, I might have drifted into a most undesirable condition. Bless the memory of my sister, who initiated in me a desire for reading and searching for things that make for a better life.

Because of the early homeschooling and motivation from my sister, I experienced a rare phenomenon in the public schools. Because of her tutoring, my knowledge accelerated. I only spent four months in the first grade and then was promoted to the second grade at midterm. After the second term, I was promoted to the third grade for my second full year of school. When I first started in school, Texas had only eleven grades. When Texas developed twelve grades, students already in school were not penalized by having to go through twelve grades, so I was able to skip the eighth grade, meaning that I was able to graduate from high school when I was fifteen years old. I was too young, too immature, and without the resources to attend college even if I had been inclined.

But my gratitude goes out to my sister for encouraging me to become interested in education and for spending endless hours tutoring me, even though she was only a bit older than me. I think my early successes built within me a quest for knowledge that lingers with me still. How do I know? My memory confirms it!

CHAPTER 4

From a Flood to a Drought

In 1934, we lived on a farm between the small town of Crandall, Texas, and a community known as Warsaw, which was simply a community stop consisting mainly of a grocery store, a community school (all grades in one building), and a cotton gin. The farms were scattered throughout a territory known as Coleman's Bottom. It was rich farmland, and under ideal conditions, the crops were very productive.

In this particular year, devastating rains occurred north of our farm near the town of Rockwall. The rain was draining into the east fork of the Trinity River, which went through the end of our property. The force of the drainage burst the dams on the river, and our farm was flooded.

As a child, my parents took me down to where our crops were flooded, and I can still see the damage rendered. The cornstalks were perhaps eight feet tall, but water was at least two feet above their tassels. My parents were devastated by the disaster.

My older brothers were having fun swimming in the floodwaters, and I wanted very much to wade as well, but my parents apparently thought it was unsafe. I can only imagine what my parents were thinking: *What will we do? Where will we go? How can we afford to really do anything?*

But my dad was a fighter—one who would tackle a chainsaw.

I am sure that he came up with a solution that he thought was the best. My mother was never one to make suggestions, knowing my father's strong will. (Perhaps this trait was passed down to his children.) She was compliant and ready to do whatever he thought was best. Most of us are strong-willed and ready to move on. We are not always right, but we are always ready!

So my dad decided that we would move back to West Texas. He acquired (I assume he bought) a Model T truck, and all that we owned was no doubt loaded onto the bed of the truck. Away we went, with all of the older boys riding atop the furniture; only my sister and I were riding in the cab with my parents. I remember very little about the adventure, only that it was long for us and frustrating for my parents. I think my dad told me that gasoline was about ten cents a gallon. We probably had a few flat tires along the way. (We never went anywhere without a few flats). The number of days it took to drive the distance is unknown, but it was an exciting adventure for me.

Once we arrived in West Texas, I do not think it rained any measurable amount for the next several years, but we saw incredible sandstorms. Often, a storm would come out of the West preceded by dark black clouds, but the closer they came, they would begin turning reddish. And then the sand would blow, occasionally for two or three days.

On our arrival in Seagraves, my dad rented an abandoned lumberyard in which we could live. We moved into every available space possible that was under a roof and enclosed. The only thing remaining was the building where lumber had once been stored, which became the town playground, where children and youth would come and climb through the rafters and flooring where lumber had been stacked. My mother worried constantly that someone would get hurt. To her surprise, nothing ever happened.

Our living quarters were crude, but there was ample space for all. My dad could really pick our residences. Memory is simply a way to relive one's life, pleasant or not. For my family, it was usually not pleasant.

CHAPTER 5

Lumberyard to a Tent

I thought life in an abandoned lumberyard was kind of unusual, but it was nothing compared to where we lived next. The 1930s were not the best time for a family in West Texas, or anywhere for that matter. Some families lived a rather decent life, but my family did not fare well. We were poor, but as a child I was not aware of it. I thought surely it was the way most everyone lived.

Just before I started first grade, my family moved into a tent that was perhaps twelve feet by sixteen feet. It was the size that might accommodate a small family, but mine was anything but that. We understood what it meant to share. Let me explain. Twelve of us lived in this small place: my dad and mother, six boys, and one girl, in addition to the two older brothers' wives and the oldest brother and his wife's small baby.

We lived on a vacant lot at the edge of town. I do not think the rent was excessive, but the togetherness was extremely so. We managed somehow, and I survived to tell about it.

As I went through first grade, I never had much space to do my homework, but just think how many tutors I had! Most people would look upon that as horrible, but the truth is, I never gave it a second thought.

How was I to know? My dad was providing the best way he

could. What did it hurt to sleep on a mattress on the ground between two older brothers? Did not everybody? Besides, I always slept warm. After all, this may have been preparing me for experiences yet to come—not necessarily the hardships that I have reported in the stories, but the impact of those hardships and how they would condition me for the years that lay ahead. I think as I looked back on the deprivations I experienced, I felt as if I may not have been as good as those who had been more fortunate. But I was a child of God, although I may not have like one.

But I have learned a great lesson: Life is not always fair, and deprivation is not a punishment. God loves each person equally, and He would not arbitrarily punish some and reward others. There has to be some positive benefit. For me it has proved itself over and over. I learned early to be a survivor.

For years I felt some shame because I was below the social level of my friends, but now I see it as a training ground for achievement. I would have never achieved what I have were it not for my humble beginnings. My early life gave me an incentive to achieve something worthy of being recognized and rewarded. I learned the hard way, and I learned early: "Life is hard by the yard, but by the inch it's a cinch!"

It was a short walk from the tent to my classroom, and I was always early. My successes in school made it better for me. I may not have been the smartest student in my class, but I was the quickest to respond to any question and the fastest one to solve a math problem at the blackboard. I was gaining confidence every day, and that was giving me an advantage in the classroom. One doesn't have to be poor to have a sister, but to have one like mine was worth it.

I don't remember much about living in the tent beyond what I have already mentioned, but I remember first grade and my teacher, Mrs. Sherrill. She was very strict, and I was a little restless in the classroom, if one wants to call it that. Furthermore, she was quick to paddle her students. I was, more than likely, over her knee more than any other student. She always paddled me with her hand and made it a practice to have all the other students laughing at the victim. It was a little embarrassing but not enough for me to stay off her lap. Looking back on it, I think I was a little bored attempting to learn what I already knew.

One day in class she called me to the front and said, "You and I are going to see the superintendent!" I was afraid of him because I had seen him whip other boys in the hallways or bathroom. So with fear and trembling I accompanied her to his office. As we went in and sat down, I was waiting for the worst.

She quietly said to the superintendent, "My student is wasting his time in my class. He already knows the first grade, and I want to recommend that he be promoted to the second grade at midterm," which was coming very soon. I do not remember the whole conversation, but the superintendent agreed, and within a few days I was a second grader. It seemed strange for me to get promoted at midterm, and the second graders seemed to resent it. But, strange as it may be, I was now one of them and competing alongside them. It may have felt strange, but it also felt very good.

CHAPTER 6

Tragic Fire: Move to Barn

One of the most tragic experiences in my parents' lives happened in about 1939. My dad had leased, to the best of my knowledge, a seven-room house about one-half or three-quarter mile just north of our town, Seagraves, Texas, on a small, sandy farm-to-market county road. I do not remember moving in, only living there. Our house was not on the school bus route, so we walked back and forth to school and town.

We had so much room that my dad subleased two rooms of the house to one family and two rooms to another family. A small orchard occupied either side of our yard, part of which he leased to a couple living in a small house trailer. Therefore, parts of three families lived in the seven-room house, while a couple occupied the small trailer home. One might say that my dad always made the most he could out of the least space. In our three rooms lived my parents, three sons, and one daughter. I never remember my mother complaining about anything. She seemed to always make the best out of bad situations.

I recall that we were awakened around three or four o'clock in the morning one day with a fire raging fiercely in the kitchen and dining area and moving swiftly throughout the other rooms. I feel certain the other tenants were experiencing rapid fire growth. My mother escaped the flames wearing only her gown, and my dad was wearing only his underwear. I had on a pair of overalls, my sister was in a cotton dress, my two brothers had only scant clothing, and a two-year-old nephew who was spending the night was in his nightgown. I have no recollection of what our neighbors were wearing, but I do remember the fire truck, which was unable to do anything because we lived about a half mile beyond the last fireplug.

My mother walked out perhaps a hundred yards or so behind the house to escape the onlookers. I am not sure what else happened that early Sunday morning. For a small child, it was the most excitement I had ever seen, but for my parents, it was the death of our home with all of its furnishings and personal memorabilia, disappeared forever.

The townsfolk came for hours on end afterward bringing bedding, tables, chairs, kitchen equipment—everything imaginable to enable us to convert our barn into a livable facility. We actually lived there for about a year and a half. When the sand blew, my mother needed to wash the dishes before we ate. It was not the ideal place to live for a few months, but we managed. It seemed this was our lifestyle—living in substandard dwellings.

A strange thing happened one day when we lived in the barn. My dad became what I thought was seriously ill. We sent for Dr. London, who came immediately. This was not the first time it had happened, and every time it did, I was petrified. Dad sounded awful. He moaned and groaned something terrible. I asked my mother, "Is he dying?" She sort of smiled and said, "No, honey, your dad is broke!"

I have wondered from my youth, what does it take to be an equal to other people? I was often embarrassed and wished that we were on the level of other people socially. I discovered later that it has nothing to do with social status, but the importance comes in the approval of the One who has created us. God places no one below another, but it takes time to wash that out of our systems. For me, it took a long time.

CHAPTER 7

The Most Difficult Years

When I have looked back over my life, I have tried to identify the most difficult times of my eighty-seven years. For me it was the times between 1938 and 1943. We lived on a farm about eight miles northwest of Seagraves, the nearest town.

The farm covered about 140 acres of sandy soil, which blew hard in the spring and yielded less-than-average crops. The house in which we lived was near an unpaved road, with some of the traffic being horse-drawn wagons. There were few automobiles then and some foot traffic.

Our house was of "box and strip" construction with no foundation. It simply was built on top of the soil. When the heavy rains would come, the water would wind its way around the sand dunes, enter our house through the back door, and go out the front. My mother would take things from the floor and put them on the beds, dresser, tables, and anything above water level. In West Texas, this much rain was rare.

We had an old barn in which we stored the corn and maize, or whatever we grew, that we usually fed to our animals. Whenever there was grass or weeds, the larger animals would feed on that. A fence surrounded the pasture to keep the animals from straying off. The farm produced very little other than food for the table, perhaps selling a little of feed grain or cotton. My dad brought money home from his work. We could have lived in the town and been as well off, but my dad was not a practical man and never shared his thoughts about much of anything.

The smaller animals, pigs, and chickens were kept in closer quarters, while the larger animals, like the cows and horses, were free to roam more widely because they were safer from the animals of prey.

Our farm produced water by way of a windmill. The water table was accessible by inserting a form of tubing that went one to two hundred feet below ground, and the water was drawn to the surface by wind power. The wheel had beveled blades that were turned by the wind, forcing a rod to move up and down with the insertion of a check valve that, when submerged in water, would lift the liquid to the surface and dump it into a barrel or watering tank.

The barrel would provide water for the household, and when the barrel overflowed, it drained into an earthen tank from which the animals could acquire their water. This is a sophisticated device, but it is also very simple in the way it provides adequate water. The water from underground was normally cold, which also provided refrigeration for keeping the milk and other ingredients cold.

This is man's use of nature to provide what humans cannot. The rest of farm life was maintained by the power of human effort, which produced sweat and muscle. To a young boy it was often boring and laborious. The time from sunup to sunset seemed like eternity.

Although I was in touch every day with God's good earth, I had not yet come to fully appreciate it. For me it was work, work, work. My only inspiration seemed to come from my mother, who was a godly woman who loved her youngest son very much. I received a great deal of inspiration from her loving touch and constant smile. Somehow I realized that to please her was all that I needed at the time. God was good, but it was shown to me through my mother. I wonder if she knows it was her faith in me that kept me going. At the time, my mother was the only God I knew. I have heard it said, "God could not be everywhere; that's why he made mothers."

What made the later years on the farm so unpleasant was the fact that my older brothers had gone to war and my sister worked in a restaurant in the nearest town. As I look back on it now, it probably was better for me than I thought it was then. I learned something about discipline that has enabled me to survive and find some measure of success in my older years. My father taught me, even though I resented it then, to never give up because some reward is around the corner.

Farm life was either hot or cold. The only thing that was constant was working sunup to sunset. When I worked in the field as a small boy, it was my job each morning to milk the cows, eat breakfast, and head to the field. We farmed with two large horses and a one-row cultivator or planter. Our horses were measured to be sixteen hands high, which made them very large. I could hardly get a bridle on them, for often they would raise their heads high when I was trying, and sometimes I would have to yell at them or kick them to get them to cooperate.

My mother had a signal when lunch was ready. She would go out behind the buildings and wave her apron, letting me know lunch was ready. I had the habit of starting my watch for her about one to two hours early. After every round I hoped I would see her. *No mother! Has she forgotten me? Never my mother!* When I was about to give up, there she would be. I would go in for lunch after I took the harnesses off the horses to allow them to rest before I went back out for the afternoon.

What made these years so difficult is that I was basically alone, a boy at the age of eleven to thirteen, working day after day with essentially no one to talk to or share life with. We were not meant to be alone. These were lonely years, miserable years, not because I carried the burden of the farm, but because I was basically alone.

In my older years, the lessons I learned were wisely used. When I grew older and changed my profession, I realized there were times

I need to be alone. But then being alone had a greater purpose to it. I suppose there are lessons to be learned at times that seemed unfair and unrewarding. I know God's plan unfolds, but why did it have to take so long?

CHAPTER 8

From the Farm to the Town

At the age of thirteen we made the long move from the farm to the city. What a revolutionary experience. I must have spent most of the day flushing the commode and turning on and off the electric lights. (The National Rural Electric Cooperative, better known as Rural Coop, had not reached our part of the world at that time.)

I could not believe it! There were no horses to harness, no cows to milk, no hogs to slop, and no chickens to feed and make sure they were in their coop by dark to avoid the coyotes. There was no need to carry water from the windmill to the house just turn on the faucet. What hasn't God thought of?

I had never stopped to think about it, but my poor mother, who was fifty-three years old at the time, had never lived in a house with modern conveniences. No more washing on a rubboard with a pot of boiling water over a wood fire. She must have thought she had gone to heaven. Where we had lived was eight miles from town down a route I had walk many times. It probably took me three to four hours at one point, but now I could do it in ten minutes! Why had not my father thought about this before?

But now, according to my father, I had to look for a job.

23

Fortunately, one came available quickly. Wacker's five and ten cent store was looking for a janitor. I applied, and the supply of labor must have been low because I got the job. I was to keep the floor and windows clean, empty the trash cans, and do whatever else the female manager wanted. The work was not very hard compared to what I was used to doing. A few young, pretty girls also worked there, and I became acquainted with them quickly and spent all the time I could visiting with them. City life wasn't bad! That is, it wasn't bad until the manager approached me one day and said very cordially, "Pete, I am not sure we can get along without you, but starting tomorrow we are going to try!"

So, I applied at the motion picture theatre and was hired to pop popcorn and usher people to their seats. They even supplied me with a flashlight that worked most of the time.

My hours started at 11:00 a.m., one hour before the movie started on Saturday and Sunday, and I was required to work through the last showing, which ended around 11:00 p.m. Then I was to sweep out the auditorium and clean the windows of the box office with Bon Ami, a product I still don't like to this day. My salary was seven dollars per week and all the popcorn I could eat. The hours were long, but the popcorn was good.

I later became the assistant projectionist, relieving the main man when he went to lunch or took a day off. My salary jumped to a whopping $17.50 a week. Otherwise, my full duties continued, with me still sweeping out and locking up. The long hours began to take a toll on my sleep, not to mention my grades.

This turned out to be an unsuitable job for me. I worked too many hours a day for too little pay, even for a boy my age. I was alone in the projection booth too much and had no social life. I worked on Sundays. Even though my mother attended church occasionally, I never had the chance to attend, even if I had been inclined, which I was not. My mind and heart were on other things that were inclined to get me into trouble. Only the possibility of my mother finding out kept me from doing anything radical. My mother was my conscience. At that time, the only God I knew was my mother or the one she told me about. God was a shadow figure for me to fear, not revere.

One of my older brothers called me one morning and said that his boss needed another hand at the service station where he worked. Was I interested in the job? I was fifteen years old at the time. I asked, "How much does he pay?"

He told me, "Forty-five dollars a week."

"When does he want me to start?" I quickly replied.

"Today!"

Goodbye, Wallace Theater! Hello, Gulf Service Station! I worked there for three years.

CHAPTER 9

My First Date

I had my first date when I was about fifteen. I had not planned it, although I had thought about it. I did not know who it would be, and I did not know when it would be. I was a little frightened to even think about it. Who would deliberately accept my invitation? I had been born in this town and knew most of the girls, but would they laugh at me if I asked them out? I did not know if I was trying to get up the courage or talk myself out of it.

Then, like a lightning strike, it happened! I didn't initiate it. I wasn't sure I was ready for it. I was excited but scared. But this was the way it happened, ready or not. A friend of mine named Tommy Oglesby caught me walking down the sidewalk, and he drove up and said, "Get in. Let's go out to the Lewellens' and see if we can get a date with the two sisters for Saturday night." It sounded like a swell idea, so I jumped into the car, my heart pounding in my chest.

We were about one mile out of town, and I began to get cold feet. "Tommy, do you really think we ought to do this?" It was so sudden! I had thought about dating for a long time, but was this the time? Why, I had the rest of my life! Had I been kidnapped to do it now? He seemed so confident about it all, but I felt so reluctant. I knew these sisters but not that well.

Perhaps they would be reluctant or even disappointed that we asked. A thousand questions came to my mind. What would I say? How would I approach them, much less their mother? Perhaps the desire to date suddenly overrode my fear.

When we arrived at their farmhouse, I was frozen in my seat. Tommy drove past the front door and around to the back door. Guests had to go through the kitchen into the dining room. Don't ask me why—that's just the way it was. When we pulled up to the kitchen door, of all things, Tommy honked his horn! I said, "Tommy, let's go!" He seemed as cool as a cucumber.

In a very short time, their mother came to the door and in a very raspy voice asked, "What do you boys want?"

I said, "Tommy, let's go!"

Tommy answered by saying, "We would like to talk with your daughters!"

The mother replied, "We don't provide curb service here. If you want to see my daughters, you will get out and come in!"

"Tommy, let's go!" I pleaded.

But Tommy opened the door, and I followed, petrified.

We followed her through the kitchen into the living room and were told, very gruffly, "You boys have a seat." I sat down on the nearest chair while she called the girls in. We acknowledged their presence. It was the first time I had ever seen them, and I wondered which one I would be dating. They were both cute, to my liking.

The mother quickly asked, "Where will you boys be taking them?"

Tommy responded, "To the Wallace Theater."

The mother responded, "Well, you had better be there because I make it a practice every once in a while to check on my daughters to see if they are where they are supposed to be."

Saturday evening, when we went to pick up the daughters, the older one said, "My mother never checks on us. We can go wherever we please."

I said, "We are going to the Wallace Theater!"

Before we had gone two hundred yards, my date leaned over and kissed me on my lips. I was utterly surprised but pleasantly pleased. My first kiss!

We went to the theater, as promised, but to this day I do not know what the movie was or who the stars were. It was still a successful date, in my opinion. We continued to date until I went into the navy, and when I came home on a ten-day leave after boot camp, I saw her every day. But when my leave was over, I did not see her for about two years.

In the meantime, my folks had moved to the Dallas area, and I learned that she had moved near Terrell. Through intense effort, I finally located her, and we dated during that leave period. I really think she expected us to get married and that I would take her back to California. I could hardly pay for the cigarettes I smoked, but I promised her I would write to her every day.

A few months after I had returned to my ship, I received an infamous "Dear John" letter from her stating that she had gotten married, which broke my heart. My caring shipmates told me the person she married was the mailman.

Thus ended the romance! I was broken hearted but lived to tell about it.

"Romance is often infatuation. Love finds its destination in your marriage partner!"

CHAPTER 10

A Promise Made,
a Promise Kept

I grew up in a rather dysfunctional family, beginning with my father. His parents' child-rearing style, which I have already written about, caused some serious disorders that were too difficult for him to overcome. His early life was extremely traumatic. I mentioned that he was given away at about the age of four. Being reared away from his mother and his siblings was extremely difficult. My father never went through analysis, but his personality exhibited severe abuse.

The way my siblings were raised had a negative effect on most of them as well. I do think that each one of them had the opportunity to alter their lifestyle, but three or four of them did not until they became older. This is not a condemnation of any of them, but it is an observation that there was perhaps an experiential tendency to walk a line a little awkwardly, especially when they were younger.

Examples are unnecessary. All one has to do is study family history to determine for oneself. As the family members became older, their conduct became much better, with a couple of exceptions. I do not wish to exclude myself, but I did live a more disciplined life than most.

One thing made a distinct difference in my life. I made a

promise, and by and large, I kept it. Let me explain the nature of the promise and the vow I made to keep it. I had four brothers in WWII, a vicious war. Many were killed, and many more were wounded. A great deal of pressure was placed on those who saw action. Two of my brothers were involved overseas, and they saw a great deal of action. One was wounded, perhaps more than once. What we now know as posttraumatic stress disorder could have been their experience or something worse. The other two saw no action, but perhaps the stress of the war and the possibility of their involvement created some kind of unfavorable disorder. However, all four became much better adjusted as they aged.

This story is not intended to denigrate my brothers or to make me look good; it is the making of a promise that was not an oath to God but, in actuality, an oath to my mother, who was the nearest thing to God in my life at the time. How else can I say it? It was a sacred moment to me! What else could it be? I made a promise to her that I would not come back from the military in the conditions that my brothers exhibited. When I walked out of the gate after I was discharged, I remembered the promise and said to my navy friend who also had been discharged, "Mel, from here on I plan to live the way I promised my mother—no more alcohol. My wife and I plan to join a church and change our habits to which I have become accustomed these past four years. I am newly married, and I want to establish a home in which we can rear children who come to know the Lord." Goodbye, navy! Hello, civilian life!

CHAPTER 11

My Navy Years

Growing up on a sandy land farm in West Texas, I appeared an unlikely candidate to join the navy. What did I know about water? I had seen so very little in my life.

I had four brothers in World War II. One was in the cavalry, one in the army, and two in the air force. All of them survived, for which I give thanks.

Early in 1948, two friends of mine from my hometown—we will just call them Marlin and Red—encouraged me to go with them to Abilene, Texas, in order to join the navy. I had always wanted to see the world, and this appeared to be my chance. My parents were agreeable, so off we went, excited about a new adventure. When we arrived in Abilene, we went to the recruiting station to enlist. We were told that in order to join the navy, we had to be eighteen years old. Two of us were seventeen, and we did not have a permission slip from our parents.

Then, a bright idea came to our minds! Why not go to Houston and join the merchant marines? We boarded a bus headed to Houston very excited about our new plans. Different service, same ocean! When we arrived in Houston, we went immediately to the recruiting office, not knowing the requirements. Again, we were told the same story—we had to be eighteen years old.

We had come to the end of the line, and we had run out of money. There we were, "landlubbers" in a foreign land, with no money. One of the boys telegraphed his mother asking her to wire him some money, which he said he would share with us. We waited near the telegraph office for what seemed an eternity without results.

We huddled to see if we could come up with the next brilliant idea. After a short time, we decided to hitchhike from Houston to Amarillo because the other boy with us had two sisters and a brother in Amarillo from whom we could sponge for a few days. (It is desperate to be penniless in a strange land.) So we caught random rides back out to the edge of Houston to begin our endless job of begging for rides. We stood with our thumbs out for a couple of hours with no luck. Then, bingo! Marlin made one last call to the telegraph office. His mother had wired him the money.

We spent our last few shekels for bus fare back downtown, picked up the money, and bought bus tickets to Amarillo. It was perhaps an eight-hour journey. Once there, we were among friends and family. Panhandling among Red's family was easy and lucrative. We spent about a week there enjoying the hospitality of old friends.

But as all good things do, the party came to an end and it was time for us to head back home. This was my first adventure without my parents. I was being led by a group of my peers, and I discovered very quickly that we lacked the maturity to make the right decisions. Being wrong isn't right; however, it seemed fun to a boy of seventeen.

Back home, I was safe and sound in my mother's bed, yet I still was preoccupied with wanderlust. Why had everything gone wrong? I knew where I wanted to be, but I could not see how to get there. But within a couple of months, I was approached by two boys from a very small town east of Seagraves who wanted to join the navy and asked me to join them. I was within days of turning eighteen and more than ready to join the navy and "see the world."

A few days later, we went to Lubbock, Texas, and visited the navy recruiting station, where we met two other boys—one from Lubbock and the other from Levelland—and we five were sent to Albuquerque, New Mexico. There, we were sworn in on my eighteenth birthday, July 10, 1948. We were then given tickets to catch a train, with sleeping berths, bound for the Naval Training Center in San Diego, California. I felt for the very first time that I had matured from a boy into a man.

From Albuquerque to Los Angeles, we would take on other recruits at every stop. By the time we reached Los Angeles, we must have had three hundred naval recruits or more. In Los Angeles, we had a two- or three-hour layover before they boarded us on the oldest train I had ever seen. All of the seats were wooden, and the trip to San Diego was mountainous, at least for that train. I shall never forget that we were going up one long hill, huffing and puffing as if we were about to come to a stop. To our amazement, we were going through a beautiful orange orchard. I do not know who started it, but suddenly all of the recruits began leaving the train, running through the orange grove and filling their pockets and shirts with oranges. I found myself among the pack, huffing and puffing to catch the train before it reached the top of the hill. I have no idea what we did with all the oranges we took from the orchard, but it was an exhilarating experience as my heart pounded wildly in my chest.

When we arrived in San Diego, we departed the train and boarded buses in groups assigned by some enlisted men who looked like we wanted to look in a short period of time. We were transported to the Naval Training Center, assigned to a company, and marched to our barracks. It was our good fortune that all five of us were assigned to company 291 and were bunked very close to one another.

The next morning, we were loosely marched over to the naval clothing center and given our uniforms, most of which fit us to some degree. I was a very skinny, 145-pound, 6-foot, 2-inch young man. My clothes fit me rather loosely. I could gird my canvas belt as tightly as I needed to hold my pants up. I was very proud to receive my uniform, especially my dress blues. We were restricted to base for the first three weeks, and then we were given liberty from 5:00 p.m. until midnight, only on weekends, for the next thirteen weeks.

The second morning of our boot training, we were marched over to the base barber shop for our initial haircut. I was in an eighty-man company, and I believe it took about thirteen minutes for six barbers to cut all eighty men's hair. Many of the men cried when their curly locks hit the floor. In thirteen minutes, we all looked like sheep that had been sheared. It was not a beautiful sight. Since it was July when I was inducted and the naval base was near the ocean, our heads blistered something awful.

One of my pleasant surprises came at the rifle range. We were using M-1 rifles trained at a target perhaps two hundred yards away. A person spotting would either wave us off, saying what in navy jargon would be a word not used in everyday speech to mean that we had missed the entire target or would give some signal that you we had hit the target with some accuracy. I was pleased to come in second place out of eighty men. My original targets on the farm were rabbits, hawks, or rattlesnakes, but my early use of a rifle paid off.

When I was given my first liberty to go into San Diego, I went with the rest of my famous fivesome, all of us in our dress blues. One of the first mistakes I ever made was with the other members of our group: we went into a tattoo parlor, and each of us had the same tattoo put on our lower left arms. The tattoo was an eagle with spread wings, and in the space across his legs was written, "U.S. Navy." All of it covered a five-point star with the word "Texas" written on it. It proved to be painful and bloody but cool. What I did not exactly know then is that when you get a tattoo, it is forever. That event happened seventy years ago as of July 10, 2018.

Much more will be told about my navy career over the next few pages.

CHAPTER 12

US Navy Years

Pollywog to Shellback

The navy is chock-full of myth and tradition, and what happens at sea can appear to be very strange. The line-crossing ceremony might just be the most interesting of all naval traditions. No one is really sure when or how this line crossing, also known as the Order of King Neptune, came about, but it was at least four hundred years before Western seafaring.

I experienced this ancient ceremony on a cruise from Long Beach, California, to Panama in the year of 1949. We were sailing south around the coastline of the Galapagos Islands when the ship cut its power in the beautiful blue waters just over the ceremonial line of the equator, and the ceremony began.

All the crew, officers and enlisted men, assembled at eight o'clock in the morning on the bow of the ship, dressed only in white navy trousers, with no tops or shoes, to begin this time-honored ceremony. The Shellbacks (those who had been across the equator) were about to initiate the Pollywogs (who had not been across the equator). This ceremony cannot truly be explained, only experienced.

The Pollywogs, numbering in the hundreds, were all assembled at the bow, awaiting the most bizarre experience of their lives. We were ordered to get on our hands and knees, one person behind the other, circling far down the starboard side of the ship to begin this ancient order of the deep.

The Shellbacks, numbering somewhere around one hundred, were standing on either side of the Pollywogs, each holding perhaps a three-foot-long object made from sail canvas that was round and stuffed with kapok, a substance stuffed in a life jacket to ensure its buoyancy, and then soaked in saltwater overnight to enable its evil usage—whacking the Pollywogs on the posteriors as they crawled toward the stern of the ship, some 684 feet away.

So the Pollywogs began their seemingly endless journey of crawling on their hands and knees, going from one absurd exercise to another for a period of about four to five hours, with few breaks. Finally, there was an encounter with a person dressed as the "Royal Baby." I cannot, for the sake of propriety, describe this portion of the ceremony. It was rather gross but not indecent. If I were to tell it in exact words, you would understand it but probably not agree with it. The US Navy would not allow anything indecent to be done but might agree to provide some good, clean fun, even if it were ridiculous.

As I remember it, the next event involved a brief respite with the Royal Chaplain. The event was labeled as "two minutes of sympathy from the Royal Chaplain." This appeared to serve as some relief from the torture of the earlier experiences, but Pollywogs were only to be hit with a cattle prod.

There were other surprises along the way, which time has generously erased from my memory. But the last experience has stayed with me for the last (almost) seventy years. The Shellbacks had constructed a canvas tank on the fantail of the ship, perhaps ten feet by ten feet, at least ten feet high and ten feet deep. When we left Long Beach, the cooks would dump their daily garbage into the tank. At the time of the ceremony, the garbage was at least seven or eight feet deep with kitchen scraps and whatnot.

The last act was to place each Pollywog in a chair and flip him over backward into the sour mix inside the canvas tank. Once this was done, the Pollywog had been converted into a Shellback, and he could take a shower or dive off the boom into the briny deep to cleanse himself from the humiliation of the day.

Thus ended the grand initiation!

CHAPTER 13

First Cruise to Asia

My first cruise to Asia was most exciting. I had joined the navy to see the world, and I could not think of anything more exciting than visiting many of the island groupings and to see and witness for the first time a culture I had read about and longed to visit but never thought I would see.

I had been aboard ship for about three or four months when we received our orders to set sail for the Hawaiian Islands and points east. Traveling from Long Beach, California, to Honolulu took approximately five days. The weather was terrific, and the dolphins were playing off both sides of our ship. The speed of our ship was a lazy twenty knots an hour. Life was beautiful. My duty was outside, up in the superstructure. Boy, was I glad I had joined the navy!

On the fifth day, we were steaming past Pearl Harbor. Suddenly it dawned on me that, just a few short years earlier, the Japanese had suddenly and without warning attacked the island from different directions, wave after wave, with bombs, torpedoes, and other destructive weapons in the process of destroying our naval fleet. It was a somber moment and a time of serious reflection. I tried to picture Battleship Row and perhaps where the Arizona was berthed, as well as the many ships that were destroyed or damaged. I remember the emotions I felt as we cruised past this historic harbor.

But my emotions changed dramatically when we pulled into one of the city piers and moored. We could hear the music coming from the ukuleles, and as we got closer, we could see the hula dancers in their grass skirts, with their hips flowing gently to the sounds of the ukes. I had dreamed of this place, never knowing I would one day be there to see it. My emotions stirred my soul. *Am I actually here?* The palm trees were gently swaying in the breeze, and the flowers painted the landscape with so many beautiful colors. For just a moment, I thought I had died and my body had been transported to this island heaven.

In a few short hours, it was announced that liberty would begin at 5:00 p.m., and we should report back no later than midnight. We had changed our uniforms from dungarees to undress whites.

When liberty was announced, men were dressed and ready, waiting for the officer of the deck to open the gangplank. Men began crowding their way down to the pier to set foot on soil after five days at sea. I cannot describe the feelings I had when I first set foot on Hawaiian soil. It was a far cry from Seagraves, Texas.

From where the ship docked, Waikiki Beach wasn't too far. I am not sure I had ever heard about it, but for sure, I would never forget it. At the time there were only two large hotels on Waikiki Beach. One was the Royal Hawaiian, and the other was the Sheraton Waikiki. I have gone back to Honolulu and the islands seventeen times since then, and the hotels are now numerous and immense. It looks as if everyone was as impressed as I was and has made the islands into a vacation paradise. It has been and will always be my favorite retreat.

After a few days, we sailed out of the harbor for nine more days of blue water sailing, heading for Yokosuka, Japan. Upon our arrival, after having lived through World War II and seeing the Hawaiian Islands in all their splendor, Yokosuka seemed a thousand years behind Honolulu.

It was a city mired in ancient buildings and primitive

transportation. The gift shops were filled with cheap souvenirs. I suspect it was much like it was before the war.

We would often travel by train to Yokohama or Tokyo to experience larger and more developed cities. In Yokosuka, the transportation was usually provided by pedicabs, which consisted of a bicycle hooked to what looked like a rickshaw. In the larger cities you would see pedicabs and taxis often fueled by charcoal. Yokohama had more to offer the servicemen on liberty than the smaller towns, with better restaurants, clubs, and transportation.

We must have stayed in Japan for three months or so, touring the country, forming small squadrons of armed sailors, and marching up and down the streets with, of all things, wooden pieces as decoys for guns as a show of military occupation.

General MacArthur, who had his office in Tokyo, was the supreme commander of all Allied Forces in the Far East. Both morning and evening, Japanese people would line the streets and bow to him when he went by. Wooden pieces and a conquering hero—something was quite artificial somewhere.

While we were in Japan, we circled all three islands that make up the country, visited most of the major cities, and often paraded through the towns as a reminder of the US occupation of a defeated country. I am sure it was humiliating for a proud people defeated in war. There was a look of disdain on their faces as we marched proudly by, reminding them of a bitter defeat.

We also visited the devastated cities of Hiroshima and Nagasaki, ghost shrines to a nuclear war. Theirs was a once-proud people humbled by the might of thunderous and fiery explosions. I walked the grounds of both cities, where there was not a twig of greenery four years after the drop. I saw cartons of soft drinks with all of the bottles were melted together without shape. As far as the eye could see in any direction, there was no sign of new growth, and large steel beams were twisted like pretzels. There was no sound, simply silence, where people once trod and traffic was congested—a silent reminder that war is extremely devastating. What I saw was a picture of utter destruction where at one time people and industry were evidence of God's presence. I shall never ever forget it! May the grace of God Almighty never allow it again.

Next Stop, Hong Kong!

We headed southward from Japan and passed within sight of Okinawa, where one of the toughest and bloodiest battles was fought before the invasion of Japan proper. It stirred within me the remembrance that one of our neighbors' sons had been killed on Okinawa. It was a sad day for the whole community when the telegram came: "I regret to inform you that your son, Ira Joe Allen, has been killed in combat." All of this occurred not too long after another telegram had come to another farmhouse less than one mile away: "We regret to inform you that Raymond McDaniel has been killed on Iwo Jima." The scars of war run deep and wide.

We were on the way toward the British colony on the mainland of China known as the province of Hong Kong when the water began to become turbulent. Before long, we discovered that we were in the grasp of a very serious typhoon (called a hurricane in Atlantic waters). The ship began to roll and pitch. The farther we went, the rougher it became. After a few hours, the ship was moaning and groaning as it encountered rougher and rougher seas. I had never been in a full-fledged typhoon. All of the main deck had been cordoned off to prevent anyone from going topside. Huge waves tossed onto the superstructure, and the ship groaned as it rolled and tossed. This storm of epic proportions lasted for five days. To be honest, it was a little hairy!

Finally, the waves began to subside, the winds died down, and we were back into relatively normal waters. As we sailed into Hong Kong Harbor, I was amazed at the number of sampans we saw. Most of them were small fishing vessels with an awning covering the top of the small, Asian-style fishing boats. Why "Asian-style"? I suppose it was the first time we had been in Chinese waters and had seen anything with a dragon head on it.

Several of my buddies commented on the fact that this was a totally different experience from any they'd had before, even though some had been aboard the ship before I was and had sailed in different waters. Hong Kong had been a British province for quite some time, but discussions had begun about returning it to the Government of China.

After having been at sea for quite some time, and especially after experiencing the typhoon, we were unable to set up mess tables for our food. So we simply went by the galley and picked up a sandwich for every meal and usually ate standing up or sitting on the deck in and around the galley.

When we arrived at Hong Kong and received our first liberty, several of us went to a restaurant in the Hong Kong Hotel for what we thought would be a lavish dinner. But being ignorant of the menu and Chinese food, each one of us, after a brief conversation, decided to stick with the tried and true—we ordered a steak with six fried eggs. Never have I eaten a meal that tasted so good. (What the meat was, though, I have no idea.)

I found Hong Kong to be a fascinating city. Since we were ignorant of Chinese history and culture, we hardly knew what to do or where to go except for doing sailor things, about which I will not go into detail.

The mode of transportation was strictly rickshaws. The architecture I noticed was mainly of the European or British variety in the business district, but in the residential areas it was a mixture of stucco apartments or wood with bamboo interiors. I really do not remember much about anything else. I do remember the fishing boats (the jargon for them was "junks"). The outlying islands, which were plentiful, were all off-limits to enlisted men. I supposed they housed the more affluent population and officer's quarters. We were there only five or six days, and then we hit the ocean again for even more adventures.

A Year in the Philippines: One Winter

We arrived in the Philippines on my sister's birthday, November 24, 1949. Sailing into Manila Bay was a somber experience because the route took us between the islands of Bataan and Corregidor, which took my mind back to the events of 1942 when the Japanese seized control of both islands and the infamous "death march" was conducted. The American prisoners were forced to march a considerable distance, all while many of them were starving to death and others were dying from diseases, the heat, or other causes. It was a merciless trek in which the Japanese acted so inhumanely.

I had forgotten all that I had read about the death march, only recalling that it seemed to be the first great atrocity of the war. I sat on the edge of my forty-millimeter director (battle station duty) simply because it was a quiet place where I could reflect on the horrors of this situation without being disturbed. The seas were quiet, and the weather was warm (it was the Southern Hemisphere's summer).

We cruised past Subic Bay (home to a US naval base) and into Manila Bay, a few miles south of the city of Manila. I have never known why I get all the breaks, but it so happened that Manila was off limits to enlisted men because of some fracas that had taken place when the USS *Toledo* had been anchored there.

Therefore, the only liberty port available was just onshore of where we were anchored, known as Cavite City. It was, in navy lingo, the armpit of the world. The town was small and dirty, and we could smell it long before we got to it.

It was so bad that it is difficult to describe. With dirt streets, hogs running loose, and sewers overrunning down the sides of the streets, the smell was horrific. We had two choices: 1) spend all of our time aboard a ship that was not air-conditioned, or 2) go into Cavite City where there was, at least, a cold bottle of beer. It was a toss-up. But boredom aboard ship for two or three days drove us ashore for a few hours. Needless to say, having only two choices for three months made our time there seem like eternity.

Besides that, our compartments were so hot that we often took our mattresses topside to sleep, only to wake up the next morning to discover that, during the night, the stacks had been blown to clear out the soot. As a result, we were covered with it, calling for a quick shower before the breakfast "chow call" was bugled.

Do you see why getting underway three months later was an experience of earthly heaven?

CHAPTER 14

A Taste of War

On June 25, 1950, the North Koreans invaded South Korea as an act of aggression. The invasion, as I understand, was totally surprising and tremendously devastating. No doubt there was a desperate appeal for military support. I was never told exactly how we became involved, but here is my story from the beginning.

I was serving aboard the USS *Helena* (CA-75) moored in our home port of Long Beach, California. We had just returned from a lengthy tour of Asia, and our command had established three consecutive leave parties, allowing the crew to visit their homes for a specific time frame. Leave party number one had gone and returned, and the second leave party was on their time away at the beginning of the conflict. I had signed up for the third leave party but was unable to take advantage of it because the second leave party was recalled, and we began to make preparations for another trip abroad, this time for combat. I do not remember exactly how I felt, but we were caught up with an uneasy feeling because most of us had never seen action.

After all the preparations had been made, such as taking on rations and ammunition and whatever we needed to face the enemy, we worked diligently to see that our ship was in the finest condition possible for what may lay ahead. We were given orders around the first or second week of July to get underway to meet other vessels of all types somewhere east of California, combining Cruiser Division Three with perhaps one hundred other ships to form a task force heading toward Korea.

We had been at sea for several days when our command decided to stage a man-overboard drill. This drill was always conducted in the same manner. One of our crew had constructed a dummy, known as Oscar, from the material that was stuffed into our life jackets to ensure its floatation. When the signal came, someone would throw old Oscar over the side while someone else would yell, "Man overboard, port!" or "starboard," as the case may be. The ship would turn in the needed direction to keep the ship's propellers from hitting Oscar. A lifeboat with crew would be lowered into the water, and the boat would *putt-putt* out to the spot where Oscar was floating, rescue him, and return to the ship to be hoisted back to the deck, where Oscar would be given immediate attention.

Thus begins the most horrible personal story of my navy career. During this particular devastating event, I was assigned to be the JV phone-talker on the bridge, where the ship's command was stationed. My phone was connected to perhaps three or four other duty stations, including the lifeboat station involving the rescue of Oscar. When the dummy was thrown over the side, the familiar shout was heard: "Man overboard, starboard!" Immediately our ship turned starboard, as did every ship in the task force, synchronized by Central Command.

The lifeboat station said in their phone, "Bridge, Lifeboat! Request permission to lower the boat!"

I said, "Bridge to Lifeboat, I have had no word from the officer of the day!"

Repeatedly, the lifeboat phone talker said, "Bridge, request permission to lower the boat."

"Lifeboat, wait a minute," I replied. "I have had no word."

Again, two or three times, he made the same request.

Finally, I said, "Lower the boat!"

Immediately, our ship's captain stormed onto the bridge and shouted, "Who ordered the lifeboat to be lowered?" My heart leaped to my throat! (I had created the most lethal situation in my whole life!) Someone had broken military law, and—oh no—it was me. I ordered the lifeboat to be launched when only the ship's captain had the authority to do so. I could have soiled my dungarees, but I didn't. I did not say a single word. I knew that my name, rank, and everything else had gone down the tube. I waited for the next salvo. The officer of the day summoned me and said, "Call down to the lifeboat crew and ask who ordered that lifeboat to be lowered."

My goose was cooked! What could I do? Trembling to the bottom of my feet, I said into the phone, "Lifeboat, who ordered that boat to be lowered?" To my utter surprise, upon hearing what he said, I responded to him in a stern voice, "What do you mean, you don't know?"

Thinking I was an officer, he said, "Sir, I do not know!" With that, I felt a slight reprieve. I reported what he had told me to my superior. Everyone on the bridge was in absolute turmoil. What was going on? I was a wreck! I had given an order that I had no authority to give. No one else knew—and at that moment, I was not about to tell.

I felt terrible. I said to myself, "Pete, surely you are not that stupid!" But I had been. What should I do? Confess and take the punishment? What would they do to me if I did? Who would be the fall guy if I didn't? The lifeboat phone talker? My head was spinning. I was out of control. I decided to lay behind a log for a while and see what happened. To my amazement, nothing did!

When my duty was over I went to my compartment, silent as a lamb. I did not dare to tell even my closest friend. I waited and waited for several days, but nothing ever happened. What would I have done had someone else been court-martialed? I really don't know. I would like to think I would have spoken up and taken the punishment, but I am not sure. My conscience troubled me for years. Who would I tell? What would happen two, five, or ten years later?

It seemed better to forget the incident and let sleeping dogs lie. But what if someone else was punished for what I did and kept silent? What if my parishioners found out? I like to think that, under fear someone else would be punished, I would have confessed. It sounds good.

This incident taught me a great lesson. Be honest. Confess and take the punishment. Don't let someone else suffer the punishment you should have suffered. As it was, no one suffered because of my stupidity, but I resolved never to repeat the same crime.

Once that incident was over, it was back to the war. I figured it would be a cinch compared to not following the correct procedure. The navy is great, but the penalties can be severe. But as long as one follows protocol, everything flows smoothly.

The task force arrived in Pearl Harbor five days after leaving Long Beach. After two or three days of refueling and taking on stores and ammunition, we set sail for Japan with our destination being Sasebo, where there was a fairly large harbor capable of handling a large fleet with fuel, stores, and an ammunition depot for us to come in occasionally to restock our supplies, as well as to provide two or three liberty opportunities, port and starboard, for the crews. Liberty was usually crowded and rowdy. If you keep a sailor at sea for thirty days at a time, where there are no women or booze, he tends to develop a wild side. The shore patrol officers were plentiful and busy.

Upon arrival in Korean waters, we met our sister ship, and the flag was transferred to our ship, placing us in command of the entire fleet on the East Coast of Korea. I am not sure if our jurisdiction extended farther than that or not.

As far as I experienced, our primary responsibility was patrolling the east coast of the northern part of the Korean Peninsula. We were regularly involved in destroying shore batteries up and down the coast, as well as destroying dangerous mines that had been dumped into the ocean by the train loads. Mines would break loose from the pack and float out to sea, risking damage to the fleet of ships up and down the coastal region. Our ship had a crew of US Marines on the bow equipped with M-1 rifles, whose sole duty was to blow up the mines. Our ship, being the flagship, usually had a minesweeper off our bow to run interference for us, but several of the ships that were directly exposed were damaged, often with several casualties.

Our ship never hit a mine, but we were hit a few times by the shore batteries; we had no casualties but a few were injured. The shore batteries were usually very deceptive. In one instance, the North Koreans had perhaps a five-inch gun mounted on a railcar within a cave. They would bring the mounted gun to the front of the cave, fire it, and then immediately roll the rail car to the back of the cave where it was impossible for us to knock it out due to the trajectory of our shells. One day after we were struck by a shell and unable to effectively return their fire, we sent a call out to Japan for the air force to send some of their F-80 dive bombers. These planes would circle above the gun locations, and when the railcar would come out to the mouth of the cave, the F-80 would dive and drop an incendiary bomb in the cave, thus effectively destroying the gun placement.

This sort of warfare would continue for about a thirty-day period, we would proceed to Sasebo for refueling and replenishing, and then we would go back out to the same duty. There were times when we were forced to rescue troops who had been backed into a small peninsula. We would cover them while landing crafts went in to rescue them, and we would take them farther down on the main peninsula and let them fight their way back up to where they had been.

Special Mission

On one occasion, our ship was chosen for a special mission. The reason was unknown to me. We left the other ships and headed north beyond the border of North Korea adjacent to Manchuria.

We traveled northward with excessive speed until we reached a region just south of the Vladivostok River that cut between Russia and Manchuria. We could see some kind of a facility, but we could not determine what it was. It must have been very valuable to the war efforts of North Korea because, suddenly, perhaps twenty or more B-29s appeared and unloaded dozens of bombs on the facility, flattening it completely. I was impressed with the mission although I did not know exactly why the facility was being destroyed.

Immediately, we reversed our course and proceeded directly back to where we had been at practically flank speed. Mission accomplished—but what was it?

I have discovered that it is difficult to write about war without sounding too morbid or too heroic. I am a normal person with normal emotions, and when danger lurks, it is normal to be afraid. I have learned that the level of fear corresponds to the level of danger. If one does not properly know the level of danger, the level of fear may rise above the normal. The unknown generally raises emotions within us to an abnormal degree. To be blatantly honest, not to know the extent of the danger is to fear it abnormally.

On one occasion, we were ordered to the Taiwan Strait to stop a possible invasion of the Nationalist forces against the Communists. No action was required.

After several months, we were ordered home for a period of rest and recuperation.

CHAPTER 15

Early Years of Marriage

I am not exactly sure of how and when I first met the woman who later became my wife. I had known members of her extended family for several years before we met. My wife, Eppie June Freeman, was reared on a small ranch near Quemado, New Mexico. She would make occasional visits to Seagraves, Texas, my hometown, to visit her relatives, although I never had the opportunity to formally meet her until several years later.

She attended a rural school for a while with some of her kinsfolk several miles from Seagraves. It was a rather strange coincidence that one of her sisters, Bobbie, lived in Seagraves and dated one of my brothers, and when he enlisted in the military, they married before he shipped out to Watton, England, with the Eighth Air Force. Bobbie and I became great friends several years before Eppie and I met.

Our first real encounter came when I was home on leave from the navy and stopped off at Hurley, New Mexico, to visit with my brother and sister-in-law, and Eppie was there. The next time we met was in Dallas when I again came home on leave and my brother and his wife were also in Dallas visiting my parents. Eppie and I went on a couple of dates while I was home and again when I visited them in

New Mexico on my return to California. A few sparks flew between us, yet I never felt the romance held real promise.

Boy, was I wrong! It is all still a swirl! It happened so fast that I still can't fully explain it. But the first thing I knew, she was on a bus heading to the Arizona–California state line, and a navy friend of mine and his wife were driving me to meet her at a bus station in a place named Salome, Arizona. We arrived there around one o'clock in the morning of January 12, 1952, and found a justice of the peace shortly thereafter. We woke him up and procured our marriage license, and then he performed our ceremony. We were quickly on our way back to Long Beach, California—as husband and wife! I was twenty-one, and Eppie was eighteen. If this happened any way other than I have explained it, you tell me!

I had to report to my ship by eight o'clock the next morning, so Eppie spent the day with Shirley Kinder, and when I received liberty that afternoon, I went to meet my bride. I frankly can't tell you the sequence of events for the next couple of days. But within a short time, Eppie had found us a small apartment to rent. I say it was small because I could stretch out my arms and touch both sides of the apartment at the same time. It was an elongated room, perhaps twenty to twenty-five feet long, with a sitting space, kitchen, dining room, and bedroom all in a row. It was cozy, but it was not my idea of what home was supposed to look like. But, at my navy pay grade, it was the only home I could afford.

We lived there for two or three months. I needed to be at sea for about a week, and when I returned, Les Hardesty, one of my shipmates, called his wife, and she said, "Is Pete with you?"

He said that I was, and Becky replied, "Tell Pete not to go home. He doesn't live there anymore!" While I was at sea, Eppie had rented a small (but not *that* small) apartment next door to Les and Becky Hardesty. This arrangement resulted in a long and fruitful friendship that outlasted Eppie's life and goes on even until today. I still get Christmas card from them postmarked "Eugene, Oregon."

We lived in that apartment until I was ready to be discharged from the navy. I was transferred to the Naval Departure Center in San Diego, California, to await my release. Eppie went by bus to Apache Junction, Arizona, to await my arrival within two weeks.

After we remained there with her folks for a few days, we boarded a bus bound for Plains, Texas, to visit one of my brothers and his family for a couple of days before they drove us on to Seagoville, Texas, to visit my parents.

Before we arrived in West Texas, my brother had brokered a job for me with Shell Oil Company in Denver City, Texas. Only a few days after we had driven to Seagoville, Shell called and advised that they wanted me to report to work within a few short days.

We returned to West Texas, and as requested I reported to work in my first civilian job after being discharged from the navy. I was excited about having a job with a regular income, and I was quasi-excited about becoming a welder. Although I was basically pleased with the company, I felt uneasy about where I was placed and the level of security and promise the position offered me. My interests seemed to point in a different direction. I felt that I was more interested in a career than a job.

But obviously it was going to take more time for me to figure out my future. In the meantime, I needed to hang onto the job.

When I was discharged from the navy with a new wife, my priorities changed. When Eppie and I moved to Plains, the first thing we did was to get established in a church. Although we were inexperienced, our hearts were leading us in new directions. The pastor of the Methodist church quickly asked me to teach a young person's Sunday school class. I said that I would and immediately felt spiritually confirmed. How do I know that? Because I did!

Regardless of how I felt about my new job, I felt better about myself. Career employment took on lesser importance, but growth in the Spirit leaped in gigantic proportion.

Gradually, I felt that I was turning a corner. Employment was a way to pay my bills, but accepting greater spiritual responsibility was a way to honor God and live my life.

CHAPTER 16

From Heavy Cruiser to Oil Refinery

Eppie and I rented a garage apartment until we could try to find some better housing. One of the first orders of business was to purchase an automobile. The nearest automobile dealer was in Brownfield, Texas, some twenty-five miles away. My brother took me there, and I found a fairly clean 1946 Chevrolet. I arranged a loan with an installment plan and drove away in the first automobile I had owned since I had joined the navy.

The next Monday I arrived at my new job, excited about learning how to weld with both arc and gas. Little did I know that it would be months before I could use anything but a cutting torch. Welding is an art, and one does not learn an art in a week.

Oil was big business in West Texas, as well as in other regions. Oil was discovered around Denver City in the late 1930s and early 1940s. Many cotton farmers went from rags to riches literally overnight.

I am not talking about light duty here because welding was hard and the hours were long. I did not have to be rocked to sleep every night. The dangers were ever present. We were constantly around high octane fuel. Any spark in the wrong place could set off an explosion.

Every day was different in the workplace, but at lunchtime it was routine. Everyone brought his own lunch, and the rush was on to get to the dining area and start our daily domino game while we ate. The competition in dominos was fierce, and the meals were routine. There was nothing to brag about in the lunch pail but much to brag about after the games.

But when the whistle blew, it was back to work. One day the competition was so fierce in dominos that one person completely forgot to eat his lunch. The friendships made there have lasted forever. I still think of the crew every once in a while although it has been well over sixty years, with much water under the bridge.

Over all, Shell is a fine company with good benefits. But, in reality, I was not looking for simply employment; I was looking for a life.

CHAPTER 17

When My Life Began to Change

One of my older brothers and his family lived in the same town where Eppie and I did, the same county where I had been raised, and it was delightful to be near them. He was the one brother I related to the most when I was growing up.

Because of my upbringing, I felt a strong need to relate to my parents' church, although my brother was disappointed that I did not attend the church of his choice. The first Sunday after we had settled in, we visited the First Methodist Church in Plains.

The pastor, Reverend Finis Pickens, an older gentleman, greeted us with warmth and genuine hospitality. He was not the finest preacher I had ever heard, but he was the sweetest man I could ever find to nurture me in my faith journey.

My wife and I decided to join the church on a profession of faith and to be open to whatever God had in store for us. I was tremendously excited to take this step toward becoming a disciple of the Lord Jesus Christ even though I was ignorant of what it was going to take and perhaps a little reluctant to fully commit myself. This was a major step for me, but I was not quite ready to commit myself fully. God's grace was at work in me, but it took a few years for it to come to fruition.

Within two or three weeks, I was asked to teach a children's class. I readily agreed and began to read and study the material, ignorant though I was. I could not remember ever opening the Bible seriously and trying to understand the will of God for my life, much less for the lives of the young people under my tutelage. I was a little uncomfortable at first for I needed to experience it before I could understand how to teach it. I am sure I was totally inadequate, but the children tolerated me decently.

The class experience went on for several months before I was asked to take other leadership roles in the church. The church was filled with senior adults, and I am sure they welcomed fresh blood. The church grew in its importance to me. The pastor was giving me more credit than I deserved. I enjoyed the attention he gave me, but I felt that I was not growing in the faith as I had envisioned.

An issue arose at my workstation with Shell. I was working with a hardened group of oil company employees who were not on the same page with me. The language was undesirable, and the employee work standards were below what I expected. I discovered that I had begun to emulate them instead of practicing my new spiritual experience. I felt uncomfortable, yet I relented too many times. This was troubling for me. How could I maintain my faith in an atmosphere of frivolity? This has been an age-old problem with the yearnings of people of faith and people who are not interested at all or who ridicule others for their position. Shell Oil began to become worrisome for me, but for the time I could not even think about leaving the company. To give up a salary for the unknown takes a lot of thought, courage, and a full measure of hope. It is a "God thing" to go from something to nothing. But God has never failed me! When we learn to trust Him in all things, we can live a secure and fulfilled life. To me, this was the beginning of Easter!

CHAPTER 18

Decision Time Cometh

Life does not wait for a person who is misplaced. Since my youth, I have had the dream of acquiring a college education. But my dream never seemed to come to fruition.

When I was discharged from the navy, I banked my hopes on the fact that I could possibly attend under the GI Bill. But time got away from me, and I was facing a critical deadline. My discharge papers said that I must be enrolled in a college or university before May 28, 1955. The problem was that I could find no college that started that early. Also, I had received the sad news that my mother's cancer was beginning to accelerate, and she had perhaps only six months to live. So I decided to sell my home in Plains, leave Shell, move to Dallas, and attend the American Barber College. Afterward, I could work with my brothers and be near my mother. It was a risk, but I really needed to be near my mother during her last days. School was important, but being near my mother was a necessity.

A college education was a pipe dream now that reality had set in. My home sold quickly, with a handsome profit. I encouraged my father to build me another home in Seagoville, just around the corner from where my parents lived.

I searched the nearby colleges and universities but found none that began before or on May 28, 1955. I had two brothers who were barbers, so I enrolled in the American Barber College in Dallas to acquire my license. After six months, I graduated from the college and joined my brothers in a three-chair shop aptly named Robertson Brothers Barber Shop.

For several months, being with my brothers was rewarding. They were both journeyman barbers, while I was yet an apprentice. But after a while the glamour wore off, and I once again felt that I was misplaced vocationally. If the truth be known, a barber demonstrates his or her skills in order to earn the almighty dollar, not necessarily to impress his fellow workers but to put the grub on the table.

The barber business is spotty during the week but excessively busy on Saturdays. My brothers and I would play a lot of checkers during business hours during the week, but on Saturdays, we might not sit down for twelve hours running. That is grueling work!

Needless to say, for someone who is often preoccupied with a call to ministry or wanting to be engaged in a college or a university curriculum, working in a barber shop can make one become terribly distracted and despondent.

The first Sunday after our move to Seagoville, Eppie and I united with the local Methodist Church, and I was immediately recruited to work with the youth fellowship that very evening. All of this went well, and I was excited.

I attended church regularly and became involved in a leadership capacity within the youth department and within the inner workings of the church itself.

My situation simply began to grow worse. I became disenchanted with the barber trade, and my life was empty and unfulfilled. I spent more time with the minister than I did behind my barber chair.

Again, the urge to attend college raised its head. I began to experience more and more signs that perhaps God was calling me into ministry. I consulted with the pastor of my church, and he took seriously the vocational struggles I was going through. After about a year of inner struggle, I was convinced that I indeed was being called to enter the pastoral ministry. From there on, my path was clear. The struggle was gone.

One Sunday morning, when the pastor gave the invitation to those who were being challenged to make any kind of decision, I walked down the aisle and met him at the altar. He asked me a simple question: "Why did you come?"

I responded, "Because above all else I want to become a minister of Jesus Christ!"

He then asked, "Do you have any reservations?"

I said, "No!" Yet, at the same time, I said to myself, *Lord, I am about to take a leap, but You had better catch me!* I did, and He did!

Suddenly, it happened. My precious mother died with her six sons and one daughter gathered around her bed. She was a woman of tremendous faith. She died attempting to sing "Amazing Grace."

My mother had always said that she wanted her six sons to be her pallbearers, and we were, with my sister walking slowly behind the casket. To our utter surprise, our father died of a heart attack three months later, on my mother's birthday.

Before I made the decision for ministry, my parents had both died; therefore I could not celebrate the moment with them. But they were there in spirit, and I knew they were well pleased. I was my mother's youngest, and I know she had great expectations for me.

With that commitment made, I began to work with the minister to enroll in the undergraduate program at Southern Methodist University—with no money but with a burning desire. But could I continue with the monetary arrangements? I had a partial scholarship but had to pay around $250 per semester out of pocket.

But with my decision to enter the ministry came the necessity to consider two things: one, where could I live that would make my travel to college or seminary relatively easy, and two, where could I perhaps find a staff job in a church that would enhance my calling and bring in a few shekels?

About that time, my current pastor, Bob Middlebrooks, shared with me that he was being considered for one of two pastorates. One was in Wichita Falls, and the other was probably First Methodist Church in Richardson. Richardson's population at that time was about nine thousand people, most of whom were east of Central Expressway.

Bob kept me informed, and I prayed fervently that it would be Richardson. It seemed that to have everything in one place would serve my needs perfectly. Richardson proved to be the place, and my move was scheduled for the first of June 1957.

Richardson became a dream come true. I was assigned some fundamental duties that grew in time, and I also found a job cutting hair in a shopping center on Saturdays. My wife and I rented one side of a duplex, and she continued working at the mailing room at SMU. School was stimulating, the church work was challenging, and life was good!

CHAPTER 19

The Beginning of a College Education

From sometime in my early life, I had dreamed of getting a college education. What at one time had been absolutely impossible became a dim hope and, finally, a reality. I always felt that I had the interest and ability to attend and graduate from a college or university. I never dreamed, however, it would be Southern Methodist University. (I have a habit of calling it Harvard of the South.)

I enrolled as a pretheological student and was assigned to the vice-president's office for ten hours a week for two years. I attended the university until I graduated with a bachelor's of arts in social studies, being directed by the seminary to the proper courses I should take before I enrolled in Perkins School of Theology.

I am extremely grateful to Southern Methodist University for years of education, mainly on scholarship. Being a future student at the seminary, I was granted generous hours on scholarship. There is no way I can ever repay that except through my service to the church, which has now lasted sixty-two years. That translates to little revenue to the university but years in the name of the Methodist Church.

I graduated from Perkins in 1965 and was appointed as pastor of the First Methodist Church in Van Alstyne, Texas. It felt so good to have my education behind me, but I realized later that my real education was still before me. Academics is one thing, but experience is another. I do not think one can have either without having both. There is valuable education on both sides of the fence. At times, one side of the educational spectrum appears to have the upper hand, while at other times experience validates one's education.

I am proud to be an alumnus of Southern Methodist University. I would not take anything for the years I spent in the classrooms absorbing data from many fields. But I am even more proud to be an ordained United Methodist clergyman who has served many different appointments with no blemishes on my record, now in a retired capacity in good standing.

I now live in retirement thanking God for every day He has allowed me to serve. And I am grateful to Him for enabling me to serve with some distinction.

I owe Southern Methodist University more than my gratitude, but my financial status forbids a large gift. My service to the church is a poor substitute for the financial support I wish I could give to SMU, but my deepest appreciation will have to do until I discover the abandoned Superstition Gold Mine in Arizona.

CHAPTER 20

My First Encounter as a Rookie

For the first few months, my responsibilities were very limited. Because of my limited experience, I was shielded from duties for which I had not been trained. I was given light responsibilities in the pulpit on Sunday mornings. I also began compiling a list of prospective members from the visitors pads, Sunday school rolls, and places like city hall where new residents put up their water deposits, along with their church preference.

Most Sunday evenings, I could be found working with youth, a responsibility I had already inherited by doing the same in two previous churches. The pastor knew what he could trust me with, as well as where I needed some tender coaching. Professional skills of the clergy needed tender supervision, but people skills enabled me to come into ministry with a measure of strength.

The church facility where we first worshipped was perhaps seventy to eighty years of age and showed signs of being in a poor state of repair. The sanctuary was a bit antiquated, and the educational area was badly in need of repair and expansion.

The congregation had already purchased some land on the west side of Central Expressway for future relocation. It was exciting to see the church body begin to plan for their future location.

The township of Richardson was at about nine thousand residents when I moved there but on the cusp of an exploding population. Practically all of the new members we received beyond June of 1957 came from the west side of Central Expressway.

Demographers learned that people who lived on the west side also went to church on the west side. Relocation was a must. What the demographers had been predicting absolutely became true.

I have discovered that when one thinks nothing can go wrong, it usually can and does. One morning when I had been in the office for only a short while, my phone rang, and when I answered it, a voice on the other end said, "My child just drowned in the bathtub. Can you come?" Without hesitation, I responded, "Sure!" This was my first emergency response to a tragedy of any kind. As I rushed out to door to go to the residence, I offered a prayer that went something like this: "Lord, I am rushing into a situation that I do not know what to do or how to respond. You must be my very presence in this home."

To this day, I do not remember anything that happened. As I went, the Lord went before me and took complete control of the situation. I know that whatever happened was appropriate, for I became friends with this household. I take no credit for whatever comfort was present and effective in that moment; the only thing I take credit for was the willingness to go in God's name.

I am writing this story to say that it became the capstone to all of my responses in emergency situations—we simply go in God's name and allow God to work through our presence. New experiences, even if they are challenging, can be the ones that make or break the way in which God speaks to us and leads us.

CHAPTER 21

First Baby! Yes ...
No ... Yes!

My wife and I had been married for about six years and desperately wanted to have a baby. After what seemed an eternity, our obstetrician informed us that a child was on the way. How thrilled we were! We read books, attended classes, consulted our doctor regularly, and waited impatiently for the grand entrance.

Finally, one morning around two o'clock, my wife awakened me and yelled, "It's time!" I said, "Are you sure?" She yelled back, "*Yes!*" So we loaded the car with everything imaginable and headed out for Baylor Hospital in Dallas—the Florence Nightingale Maternity Hospital, in particular.

I had made a few practice runs in both day and night, just to be sure. I was driving toward Baylor on Greenville Avenue at a generous speed, and when I turned right on Ross Avenue in front of what was then Sears Department Store, I saw a flashing red light in my rear view mirror.

I pulled over to the side, rather impatiently, and waited for a slow-walking, gum-chewing gumshoe to approach the car. The policeman had already pulled his ticket book from his pocket when he said, "You know that you were speeding?" I wanted to be funny and say, "Not as fast as I wanted!"

But he looked a bit impatient, so I leveled with him. "Officer, my wife is about to deliver a baby, and I am on the way to Baylor!" His expression turned ashen, and he blurted out in good police etiquette, "Follow me!" He spun his wheels getting around me, and I tried my best to stay up with him.

He turned into the emergency department of Florence Nightingale after radioing for assistance, and out came a crew of nurses, doctors, technicians, business office personnel—you name it. We were ushered directly to the delivery room. All of them disappeared into a private area and left me standing in the hallway.

About four and a half hours later, the doctor came out and said, "False alarm!" *What?* I handed my wife over to a group of people who sequestered her behind closed doors, telling me nothing; I got through an episode of *Dragnet*; and I waited for hours, anxiously waiting for the tiny cry of my newborn child, only to hear the doctor say, "False alarm"? Was my wife the victim of weight gain, or was she really pregnant?

The doctors attempted to be sympathetic. "The answers are, no, she is not the victim of weight gain; yes, she really is pregnant; but the truth is that she is not ready to deliver. So, what we are saying, Mr. Robertson, is take her home until she is ready."

So, we loaded the car, headed back up Greenville Avenue, and climbed the stairs to our garage apartment wondering if all of this was simply a joke. The signs indicated that it was no joke, but when would the baby come? You guessed it! At about two o'clock the next morning, I was awakened with the same words—softened, but just as sure: "It is time!" So, just as deliberately, we grabbed the bag, loaded the car, backed out more slowly, and headed up Greenville Avenue toward Baylor. I am sure I was driving the same speed I had been the previous day but with a cautious eye, watching out for "Jack Webb." What would I say if I got pulled over again? But there was no need to explain. I never saw him.

We made it to Baylor, and before long, Eppie was whisked into the delivery room. After several anxious minutes, the doctor came out with the joyful announcement: "It's a boy! Nine pounds, and (I believe) thirteen ounces." Thank God, all was well and healthy! We named him Stephen Andrew Robertson. His first and middle names are both biblical. There is no special implication behind the names other than their biblical roots. Both men were strong characters, and each is remembered in his own way for serving in leadership roles. Stephen was known as the first martyr after being stoned to death, while Andrew was a fisherman with a sterling character who always brought people to Jesus.

My son is now a minister, following his namesakes in scripture—and his dad!

CHAPTER 22

My Three Children

The mother of my children was sadly killed in an automobile accident in 1979. It was a horrible scene, with three dead, one not expected to live, and two with minor injuries. I was the one not expected to live, but by the grace of God I survived and am in reasonably good health, now eighty-eight years of age.

I cannot say enough to praise my children, not only because of the way they dealt with their mother's death but also by the way they have lived their lives and achieved so much in their careers.

My oldest son is Stephen Andrew Robertson, an ordained United Methodist minister who presently serves as the executive pastor of the First United Methodist Church of Frisco, Texas. Steve has served the North Texas Conference for some thirty-four years, with a perfect and effective service record. Steve has two children, Jacob and Erin, who are both employed but are considering changing their vocations commensurate with their present callings and interests. The pride of the family is Luke! Jacob and Nikki's son is a sweet young thing bordering on two years old who has captured all of our hearts.

My daughter, Lori Beth, is the middle child, and she married Alan Flores. They have two sons who are loaded with charm and talent. Both boys were diagnosed with autistic spectrum disorder very early on. Nick is the older of the two, is more social and outgoing than his brother, and graduated from high school this year, but he has four more years in high school transition classes to develop more daily life skills and to work on vocational training to increase his ability to be employed in the labor force. He is a good-looking young man who shows tremendous promise.

Sam is a more sedate young man of seventeen who is a senior this year in high school and then has four years of high school transition classes as well. Sam has a wonderful singing voice that he developed from his love of music. He has been in the concert choir since he was a freshman. Who knows? He may become a recording star down the line.

Alan, my son-in-law, works for Freeman Audio Visual, as did my daughter. Alan has thirty-five years with Freeman, directly related to the convention and trade show business.

My daughter worked with Freeman for twenty-nine years but was recently laid off because of a reduction in force. I am so proud of what she has done. She was recently hired on with a brand-new scrap metal company in Fort Worth. She has the ability to perform at the highest level and has received many commendations from her company. She has a sweet spirit and is a dedicated worker.

My third child is a son, David Page Robertson, who is connected with the United Methodist Church of the Resurrection (CORUMC) in Leawood, Kansas, and has worked with Adam Hamilton for something like twenty-four years. Dave is a great pastor and is now linked with a satellite of CORUMC located in Olathe, Kansas. Dave is extremely adept at working with small groups, athletic teams, teaching, counseling, and hosting groups in his home. Dave is a Christ-centered servant who will do anything to encourage individuals and families to become active for Christ and His church. Dave has a most gifted workmate who sings like a canary and organizes activities second to none. They are a beautiful and effective team. They have no children, but they have great fun being together and sharing their servanthood.

I could not be more proud of my children. Perhaps they received their gifts from their mother, but I am around to see them displayed. Thank God for children!

CHAPTER 23

My First Pastorate

I was licensed to preach under the supervision of the late Dr. Wesley V. Hite, superintendent of the Dallas-South district, in the fall of 1956. At the time, I felt a sense of achievement. It was my first step toward earning the role of an elder within the North Texas Conference. (In a way, I was "feeling my oats.")

I look back on it now, and it seems so trivial. But one has to begin somewhere, and this marked my beginning to "wherever." Thank God for the minor victories over the next eight years as I served on the staff of First Methodist Church as their evangelism director—and, loosely speaking, as their assistant minister, liturgist in worship, and funeral (and later wedding) conductor. I organized several adult Sunday school classes and did whatever someone could find for me to do. I also barbered on Saturday. I was a busy fellow but was rewarded enormously.

In 1964, Bob Middlebrooks, the pastor with whom I had worked for several years at Seagoville and Richardson, was appointed superintendent of the Dallas Northeast District during the final stages of a new sanctuary being built. He felt that the bishop could have delayed his new appointment until after the new sanctuary had been opened. He served in his role of superintendent, but his heart ached as pastor.

When Bob left the pastorate to become a superintendent, part of my heart went with him. We had been together in two locations for over ten years, and my mentor and I were separated, outside the womb, and I felt alone in a sea of people.

The new minister who succeeded Bob was a fine man who treated me with the deepest respect, but a relationship had been disturbed and it was impossible to reconnect in the same way. There was something of the same feeling among the congregation. Many began to turn to me because of my tenure, and I knew it was time for me to move on.

I decided to go see Bob and see if he could find me a new appointment. When I approached him with the idea, he said, "We have only one appointment open, and it is at First Methodist Church in Van Alstyne, Texas. I said, "I'll take it!" He said, "You don't even know where it is located." I replied, "I don't care. I'll take it." He informed me it was in the Sherman district and that I would have to go through Dr. Slack, the superintendent there, in order to be considered.

Bob called Dr. Slack and arranged an appointment, and I went to meet with him at the Grayson Hotel in Sherman to see if there was a possibility of my receiving that appointment. I found Dr. Slack to be rather elusive. After a couple of hours of conversation, he informed me that he would be holding a preacher's meeting in Van Alstyne the following Wednesday. He encouraged me to attend the event, but he failed to mention that I may or may not be the appointee to that charge. I decided to attend the event, just in case I was being considered.

We met in the basement of the Van Alstyne church and went through what I suppose a typical district preacher's meeting was like. I don't remember much about it, so it probably did not amount to much. After the meeting, Dr. Slack took me upstairs into the sanctuary, and to my surprise, most of the members of the official board were there, waiting to meet their new pastor. It was quite a surprise but one that I thoroughly welcomed and enjoyed. I had not ever been given an opportunity like this and considered it a unique honor. I went around and shook hands with each person there, and by the time our meeting was over, I felt as if I had struck a gold mine.

My appointment was effective on February 1, 1965. What a lucky person I was, if *lucky* was the word, to be able to serve a small-town church of approximately two hundred fifty members who were "salt of the earth" type people.

Moving day came quickly, and it was time to get Stephen enrolled into first grade, with Mrs. Ruth Spence as his teacher. Steve fell in love with her immediately and thus started a "love affair" that has lasted some fifty-three years now, if my math is correct. Ruth is now approaching one hundred years of age, is widowed, and lives alone on her farm just north of town.

Lori, my daughter, was not of school age while we were in Van Alstyne, so she spent much of her time entertaining Virginia Ayers and her father, Chili, who lived next door to the parsonage, along with Virginia's friend Joe Baker.

Our youngest child, David, was born at Baylor Hospital in Dallas, as were Steve and Lori. After David's birth, when his mother was ready for discharge, Don Flesher, the funeral director in Van Alstyne, drove the family car used for funeral transportation to Baylor to pick up mother and son. Billie Whitaker made the trip and held David on the return trip.

I have so many memories of Van Alstyne that it would be impossible to rename them. Van Alstyne would have been a great town in which to grow up. It was completely opposite of where I had been living for the previous eight years or so. I had spent my ministry on the fast track, and it seemed extremely relaxing to be able to slow down and smell the proverbial roses.

The congregation treated us with great respect and with small-town cordiality. I loved going to the church early and taking a "time out" during the middle of the morning to walk the two blocks to downtown and have a cup of coffee with the townsfolk and church members alike. City Drug was the gossip center. The main attractions at City Drug were Ruby, Vera Mae, and Sue, the employees who knew not only everyone in town but every*thing* about everyone in town.

The next daily stop was the post office. Between City Drug and the post office, I could encounter the town leaders, town gossipers, and all the community facts I ever wanted to know.

The greatest events of the year came in the fall with the annual football games. Everybody who was anybody showed up at the football games. The town went from full (home games) to empty (away games). The town carnivals were exciting, the American Legion was generally crowded, *The Leader* was well read, the churches were well attended, and the funeral home was busy two or three times a week. The town population was rather static. The announcement of a new family recreation center, or country club, was welcome news.

One of the most grueling jobs I had was writing two sermons a week. The Sunday morning sermon basically took me the better part of five days, and the Sunday evening sermon took me the better part of Sunday afternoon. Sunday was not a day of rest for me; it was a day of labor—delivering on Sunday morning and preparing on Sunday afternoon.

Most of the townspeople were generous to a fault. The Bentons provided the tennis facilities and the skating rink. City Drug became the gossip center, while the American Legion provided the watering hole. The schools supplied the facilities for just about everything, and the ministerial alliance afforded recreation opportunities for the youth.

Van Alstyne was a great place for my children. The church was the only first pastorate I would ever have. But the only thing I had become accustomed to that it did not have was a fast track for me to practice ministry. My soul longed to be back among the suburbanites in an area teeming with people and limitless opportunities. When the opportunity came two short years later, I could not resist, so I accepted an appointment where pastor meets suburbia.

(Disclaimer: I think it inappropriate to discuss any ministerial relationships.)

CHAPTER 24

Superintendent
to Pastorate

In 1977, I had been serving as the superintendent of the Dallas South District for almost four years. I had fifty-eight churches assigned to my district: metropolitan, suburban, and rural churches. The travel throughout my district was tiresome, and in most evenings I was required to be away from my family. The schedule became exhausting. I had three children still at home, and I longed to be a greater part of their lives, their school functions, and our family life.

My presiding bishop was forced to be out of town for several days to attend meetings with some of our general agencies. He asked me to meet him at the airport when he returned. When we were leaving the airport, he asked how the most recent appointments had gone. I referred to three churches in particular from which pastors had been reassigned and other pastors were taking their place. One of our megachurches needed to have its pastor position filled because the pastor had been reassigned to the faculty of our seminary at SMU. The other church was in a critical suburban area. The moves had left a church open in the northern part of our conference, near Lake Texoma. The church was Waples Memorial

United Methodist in Denison, Texas, a congregation of about twelve hundred parishioners.

It was an enticing opportunity for me that would provide some relief from grueling work on the district, as well as fill a pastoral void for which I was originally called and missed so dearly. I made my pitch for the appointment, and the bishop said that he would consider it and let me know within a brief span of time.

The bishop called me in a couple of days and said that he had approved the appointment, effective December 1, 1977, with the stipulation that I complete my charge conferences. These required my presence as the district superintendent, who was the presiding officer in every local church, as they conducted their year-end reporting along with a celebration of their accomplishments. The conference provided a way for the superintendent to congratulate them on their past year's work and present them with a challenge for the future. I cannot tell you how much it means for a congregation to celebrate its true achievements over the past twelve months and to begin a new year on a positive note. I love to play the role as a "conference cheerleader" as a local church catches a glimpse of their tremendous opportunities for the upcoming year.

Given my responsibilities for December 1977, I still had at least fifteen churches to visit in order to preside over their charge conferences, on top of preaching each Sunday morning at Waples and fulfilling some duty each day before I began my drive to the next conference.

I do not want you to feel that I was working under an unfair demand or situation. It was a God-given challenge, and I reveled in it. To be with people and to celebrate their successes is a celebration for all. Wherever people are, I feel that is where God is, and that is a place I enjoy.

I looked upon 1978 with great excitement. I had inherited a good and dedicated staff who welcomed me with open arms, and we worked together under a single purpose—to serve the needs of our congregation. Rolly Walker was serving as an assistant pastor while attending Perkins School of Theology, giving perhaps twenty hours a week of his time to various responsibilities, both assigned and volunteering.

My other clergy staff member, with remarkable gifts in every area of ministry, was Paul Cardwell. He served with distinction for years in the office as the director of Christian education for the annual conference. Paul was an invaluable resource in that field. What a pleasure it was to have someone with that knowledge and status on staff.

It was a great surprise to me that on my first Monday of work, Paul came in and handed me his letter of resignation. I was beyond words. How could this happen to me? To lose a man of such character and distinction was more than I could bear. I asked him why, and he replied that he thought every pastor should have the right to name his own staff.

After he walked out of my office, I immediately drafted a letter to him indicating that I desired his presence on our staff and that there was no one I would rather have than him. I felt that he was the best authority in Christian education within and without the boundaries of the annual conference. I pleaded with him to reconsider his resignation and join me in the work at Waples. To my great pleasure, he responded positively. He simply said that he felt he should be invited, rather than assume he still had the responsibility. I have never forgotten that experience, and it was a learning time for me.

I also inherited an experienced secretary who knew everyone connected to our congregation, and what a blessing it was to have her introduce all of her acquaintances to me. A pastor who does not know his parishioners is pastor to none.

With time came inevitable changes. One of the first staff changes came when the business manager indicated that he must resign because he was moving out of the state. This was a blow to me because I had never even seen the books. I assume he could have nurtured me along from the time I came, but my interests were on general management and my own need to be a pastor to the people and a shepherd to the flock.

Therefore, one of my first duties was to find a replacement for my business manager. After much prayer and deliberation, I decided to go after Reverend Ken Summy, who was a retired navy chaplain living in Whitesboro, Texas, not a far commute from our church. I had met Ken at a district meeting and was very impressed with his manner of dress and demeanor.

So, about midmorning one day, I drove over to Whitesboro, met Ken and his wife, and had a very nice discussion in their home. I introduced the reason I had come to see him, and frankly I was surprised at his response. He said that he was not interested in the position but appreciated the offer. I was disappointed in his response and a bit taken aback that I had been refused. (I don't take refusals lightly.) I excused myself and drove back to Denison very dissatisfied.

I took a couple of days to think about his refusal and decided that I wasn't convinced that he was that definite. There was something unexplainable about our conversation, which I replayed over and over in my head. Since I could not clear it out of my mind, I made a decision to drive back over to Whitesboro and give him one more effort. I found him outside feeding his livestock. I parked my car and walked over to where he was. We exchanged cordial greetings, and I simply said, "Ken, I need you!" And to my pleasant surprise, he said, "When do you want me to start?" Short, simple, effective!

I also had lost my student associate, who, upon graduation, wanted to go back to Louisiana from which he had come. I worked with the bishop to find a replacement. I interviewed two different candidates, after which I asked Bishop Stowe if he would appoint Carroll Caddell as associate minister to Waples. He did, and my staff was once more complete.

After about two years, Ken Summy was forced to retire, so the search was on again. My intuition led me to explore someone I had known years before at First UMC in Richardson. He had been the business administrator for the Richardson Independent School District for several years before he entered the pastoral ministry. He was currently serving as the superintendent of the Wilmer-Hutchins Independent School District, a district that had encountered much turmoil over the preceding years. I drove down to Wilmer and approached Alden "Chubby" Armstrong about moving to Denison. He practically leaped into my arms with great joy, and without hesitation he accepted the position.

So, once again, I had a complete staff and all looked well.

Wrong! Soon after, I suffered the greatest tragedy of my lifetime. My wife and I and my two associates and their wives were involved in an automobile accident as we turned off the highway and onto a street that led us to the Armstrongs' home. We were blindsided by a drunk driver who was traveling at an estimated speed of ninety-five miles per hour, killing three people instantly. Those killed were my wife and both of the Armstrongs. I was seated in the left back of the automobile, but with the car so damaged, the first responders had to remove my body through the back glass.

Of course, I was unconscious for most of three days. The physicians told my family on the first day that I would more than likely not live through the night. On the third day I was in intensive care, and my son Steve and daughter, Lori, came in to see me. I asked them where Mom was, and when they couldn't answer me, I looked into their eyes and realized that she had died.

Bishop Stowe and his wife, Twila, were on vacation in Nova Scotia, and upon learning of the accident, they came home to minister to the needs of my family and staff. What a dear couple they were!

By this time, my oldest son, Stephen, was in college in Georgetown, Texas; Lori was studying criminal justice at Grayson County College; and David was in the ninth grade. These were traumatic times within our family, but the church family and many friends provided comforting support. The larger family can enable us to survive and grow through most tragedies.

CHAPTER 25

A Marriage Made in Heaven

Some time later, I married Jane Hynds Benton on May 31, 1980, in a lovely ceremony performed by Bishop W. McFerrin Stowe in the beautiful sanctuary of Waples Memorial United Methodist Church in Denison, Texas. It was the celebration of all celebrations since I had been their pastor. I was bringing to the parsonage a new wife since my first wife had been killed the year before. The hymn that Jane and I chose for our wedding is following.

> Praise to the Lord, the Almighty, the King of Creation!
> O my soul, praise him, for he is thy health and salvation!
> All ye who hear, now to his temple draw near;
> Join me in glad adoration!
>
> Praise to the Lord, who o'er all things so wondrously reigning
> Bears thee on eagles' wings, e'er in his keeping maintaining.

God's care enfolds all, whose true good he upholds.
How hast thee not known his sustaining?

Praise to the Lord, who doth prosper they work and
defend thee;
Surely his goodness and mercy here daily attend
thee.
Ponder anew what the Almighty can do,
Who with his love doth befriend thee.

Praise to the Lord, who doth nourish thy life and
restore thee,
Fitting thee well for the tasks that are ever before
thee.
Then to thy need God as a mother doth speed,
Spreading the wings of grace o'er thee.

Praise to the Lord! O let all that is within me
adore him!
All that hath life and breath, come now with praises
before him!
Let the amen sound from the people again:
Gladly forever adore him.

The hymn filled the sanctuary as our hearts soared in the love we had committed one to the other. There was no doubt in either mind that God had brought us together and would be our constant companion.

The reception that followed was an endorsement of our union and the affirmation of the congregation that they were united as one behind our divine marriage. What a true witness it was to what God can do to those who love Him and each other.

Everything went perfectly from beginning to end. We will always be grateful to Bishop and Twila Stowe, the choir, the organist, the ushers, and others who participated.

Jane and I went out to Tanglewood Resort to spend our wedding night in one of their large tower suites. We went back to Waples on Sunday morning so that I could preach and then began our drive to Estes Park, Colorado, for our honeymoon. What an exciting moment that was for both of us. I was eager to show Jane all of the sites around the Rocky Mountain National Park, my cabin, and the friends we had come to love—but not nearly as eager as I was to be away with Jane for a couple of weeks. New, intimate relationships require a great deal of tenderness and special care, and I especially wanted to be aware of her feelings and needs. We felt we were created for each other; therefore, whatever we did seemed natural and pure.

Of course, our marriage took on special responsibilities because of our children. To develop a relationship with a wife is one thing; to learn how to relate to adult children is something else. One does not automatically assume a parental role because one has to first learn to relate as adult to adult within a family setting while also learning how to relate as more mature adults, offering whatever resources are at our command, without being superior or demanding. I think the spouse's children can be resistant to what is intended as advice. If there is an unresolved issue, perhaps it should first be discussed with the spouse, and then he or she should visit with his or her children as an intercessory action before proceeding with a designed plan. This is tedious work and requires the best of us to execute it.

Jane has two children, Kay and Bill, from her first marriage to Henry Benton, who died an untimely death in 1966. His father had started an insurance business, and after World War II he took it over. After his death, Jane assumed the management of the agency for fourteen years until our marriage, when her son, Bill, took ownership of the agency and has managed it with meticulous precision. Bill and his wife, Paula, are both in the real estate business as well. They have three children: Kathryn, who was diagnosed with Angelman syndrome at an early age; Henry, who is an attorney; and James, who is working with a private telephone company. Henry and his wife,

Hayden, have a son named George, and James and his wife, Jessica, have a son named Mason,

Kay and her husband, Bill Stuart, live in Steamboat Springs, Colorado, where they owned a grocery and wine store for over twenty years. They are both retired from full-time employment and now work part-time with SKI Corp. They enjoy their winter home but also own a condominium in Dallas, where they spend several months each year. They are a delightful couple with whom we enjoy whatever time we have together. Blending families is never an easy thing to do, but it was not too difficult for Jane and me because our children were mature and perhaps understand what it would mean to lose one's mate. There have been cordial relationships on both sides for thirty-seven years now. Living alone is not easy, while marriage provides satisfying relationships in all quarters. To get married after the loss of a spouse depends upon the love of two people and their willingness to make whatever adjustments are necessary.

After our wedding, Jane and I remained in Denison from 1980 until 1983, at which time Bishop John Russell asked me to become superintendent of the Dallas Central District, which had offices downtown in the First United Methodist Church building at Ross and Harwood. There was no district parsonage, so we bought a condominium in North Dallas, and I drove downtown every day. The Dallas North Tollway was new, and the traffic was accommodating. I could get to my office within about twenty minutes at the most. This was the first time we had lived alone since our marriage, and we loved where we lived. Life was good.

However, I missed the local church. The people at Denison had been so good to us, and being a local church pastor was the height of my calling. But it felt good being back on a district. The responsibilities between being a pastor and a superintendent are so diverse that it is exhilarating and often more challenging. I had about thirty churches assigned to my district. There was a great deal of travel involved, but most of the churches were within twenty or so miles.

CHAPTER 26

Early Retirement Years

I retired from the North Texas Conference of the United Methodist Church in June of 1990, having announced my intention to retire in February of that year. I choose not to reveal the circumstances involved in my choosing to retire, but the evidence can be documented.

Perhaps two weeks after I made my announcement, I was approached by the pastor of Custer Road United Methodist Church in Plano, inquiring as to whether or not I would be interested in joining the staff of that church. I responded that I would not be interested at that time but thanked him for asking me. Two weeks later, this pastor came to see me again and asked if I had been considering it. I told him again that I was not interested.

Another two weeks later, the same pastor approached me with his hand raised, palm facing me. He said, "Do not say a word! I have a proposition you cannot refuse!" Since the earlier visit, I had begun to think that it may be good for me to work part-time somewhere, perhaps even at Custer Road.

His proposition sounded something like this: "Look—I want you to make eight calls a week. You may take them to breakfast, lunch, or dinner or play golf with them, as long as you make eight calls a week. If eight calls are too many, make five." This proposition sounded rather appealing, so I said, "You have talked me into it." He then said that I had pleased him a great deal.

Two weeks later, he came to see me again. I said, "I have already told you that I would come to work in June. What now?" In his own persistent manner, he said, "Look, I have an associate who would like to take a sabbatical next January, February, and March. Would you even consider working in her place for those three months?" I thought, *These are winter months, I will not be playing much golf, and besides, we will not be traveling that much in the winter.* So I said, "Sure, I will be glad to do that!"

He smiled graciously and said, "That is wonderful!" I thought surely the visits were over this time. Wrong! Two weeks later, he came back and said, "Look!" (His favorite phrase.) "I would like to take a sabbatical in June, July, and August. Would you consider working for me while I am gone?" I said, "Why not? Sure!" He smiled broadly and said, "But I am going to pay you!" I said, "Yes, I think you will pay me well!" The deal was cut in February for me to begin working on the first of June 1990.

In retrospect, I could not have been happier. As it turned out, it became one the most rewarding positions I had ever had. What would I have done were it not for Custer Road? Jane and I left for a while and attended other churches, but it was never the same. So we decided to return there, and we will be there until God calls us home!

But this is not the end of the story. Some of the great moments in my ministry have come with the congregation of Custer Road. Let me share with you a few of these landmark memories.

Our first Sunday at Custer Road coincided with the grand opening of the new sanctuary. We helped open the doors to a beautiful and functional facility that has served thousands and thousands of worshippers over the past twenty-eight years.

I cannot tell you how many weddings I have conducted there or how many memorial services I have presided over. This is not a secret, but the pastor then was not inclined to preside over weddings or memorial services. To his credit, he would say to me whenever an opportunity arose, "Look, I would appreciate it if you would conduct (whichever), but if you need me to say a word, just let me know and I will be there to support you." He did not mention this in February before I said yes, but that was his standard remark after I took on the responsibility.

We had not been at Custer Road very long when the pastor came to me and said, "We are planning to build a chapel adjacent to the sanctuary." A couple in the church had offered to donate the funds whenever we were ready to begin. Then he said, "Do you mind taking on the project of selling their donated home located in Tanglewood Resort at Lake Texoma?" (Sound familiar?) I replied, "I would be glad to if the donors do not object." He said, "I have already talked to them about it, and they would be pleased."

So a few days later, I went to Tanglewood with Joe and Doris Sowell to look at their beautiful home that would soon fund the chapel at Custer Road. After assuming the responsibility of marketing their home, I contacted all of the Realtors I could locate in the Tanglewood area and set up meetings with them so they could see the property and so I could share with them the price for the home that the Sowells had suggested.

On the day the Realtors were supposed to meet, I arrived at the home perhaps an hour early in order to properly receive them upon their arrival. Within a few minutes of my arrival, an automobile pulled up in front of the home, and a tall, stately lady came up the walk, rang the doorbell, and said that she was interested in purchasing the home at the listed price with *cash*! Needless to say, the Realtors never met, and I went back to Plano with a smile.

It was then that I realized an old cliché was true. The difference between a long, skinny girl and a tall, stately girl was $300,000 in cash (a stately girl was one of tremendous resources)!

Custer Road took root in my heart and life quickly. I felt entirely at home, and the people were accepting and friendly. After almost thirty years, the people have come and gone, and some have aged and mellowed, but it is still home to Jane and me.

The church, in our time, has changed dramatically—and generally but not necessarily for the best. Culture is the modern change agent where the Bible once was. It seems that if anything changes, it is usually for the worse. (Pessimism sometimes rules). I look back over sixty-one years of ministry, and the future does not shape up with any clear optimism.

Custer Road stepped up to the plate several years ago when it invested in the seventeen acres on the corner of Custer Road and Legacy. The plot has proved its value over and over. As I remember it, Custer Road paid approximately $1 million for the property, and it has served many purposes since. When the property was purchased, the pastor played magician with the City of Plano by offering them the east end of the property for a soccer field in exchange for never having to pay taxes on the totality of the property. History will record that deal as one of the finest ever made. Beyond that, the pastor had added to the contract that if the church ever needed the soccer field for further ministry development, the no-tax clause would remain in effect. The church has used the land for many purposes that would have been difficult to find other land for in close proximity to the church.

Into every good deal goes questionable consideration. It is one I have second-guessed many times. Back in about 1997, Dr. Ron DelBene, Jane's primary consultant on the Prayer Ministry Project and one of her instructors at the Spiritual Academy in Nashville, was asked to fly into DFW Airport to be part of an all-day meeting with the pastor, Jane, and me to present to us a proposal for multipurpose usage of the seventeen acres, including things like a senior activities center and other ministry buildings, plus parking, to supplement the worship facilities that presently adorn our southern campus. A great deal of pros and cons were discussed, but it sounded terrific.

After hours of exhaustive discussion, the three of us were on our way back to the church property when the pastor indicated that he wanted no part of it. That killed the whole idea. One of the intriguing questions that has occupied a portion of my brain all these years is, what if we had decided to recommend it? Would it have been a good idea or poor judgment? Time always poses stimulating questions. I am a gambler, in a way, and I saw great possibilities when others saw stumbling blocks. I am willing to take risks where others play it safe. That is why there is so much diversity in the world. This was not a right or wrong decision; it was simply an opportunity to do something different. The richness of Custer Road's great programs and ministries lies in what has happened, not in what might have happened. In either case, you and I are richer.

But the questions that all of us must answer are, What do we do next? How faithful are we now? How can we preserve our heritage? How can we prepare for an unknown future? We are an aging congregation, and the question for me is, what can I do to give the best of myself in the time I have remaining? Experience, maturity, and decisiveness trump inexperience, immaturity, and indecisiveness every day of the week.

Retirement is not for everyone! Count your blessings, and follow the Lord in all things!

CHAPTER 27

Greatest Surprise

My ministry has been filled with many different expectations—some of them realistic, some unrealistic, many ambiguous, but most of them affirming and encouraging. Through all of them, I have been challenged to fulfill my responsibilities with honor and dignity. I admit I have been diligent about those things that were challenging and difficult and were best for my congregations.

As a receiver of surprises, I have often been skeptical and somewhat embarrassed by most. However, one surprise has surpassed them all. I shall never forget a call from the pastor of a church where I had been volunteering for the previous nine years, offering my talents and experience whenever and wherever I was called upon. I was asked to meet with a designated group of laypersons, along with the pastor. I was not given a reason or a duty, simply an invitation. I thought I had been invited to, perhaps, a work session, simply as a courtesy considering my role as a volunteer professional. Boy, was I wrong!

For months, we had been working on the concept of building a family life center that would serve multiple functions. We had been through a dozen or more phases of discussion and planning for the mixed-use facility. We had also conducted a stewardship campaign through which the building would be financed and paid for. But never had I dreamed of what I was about to experience.

After much discussion about the details, the pastor, John Mollett, directed his remarks to me, saying, "We have decided to name the structure the Robertson Family Life Center."

I was absolutely stunned! Words were hard to come by. At first, I could not believe my ears.

My first thoughts were that I had done nothing to deserve such an honor. I was simply a volunteer, like many others, and had been delighted to share my expertise for the simple pleasure of working alongside other volunteers.

My response to the group, as far as I remember, was something like, "Usually, you name a building after someone who has offered to give a relatively large sum of money toward its construction." I was honored by the thought but honest in my response. We were talking about a beautiful building requiring a large sum of money to build, and to honor a generous donor seemed to be the most reasonable way to proceed. I was extremely flattered but pragmatic in my response. If I had been the pastor, under the circumstances, I would have been looking for Mr. Got Rocks!

But this was not the thinking of the group. I questioned their decision, but there is nothing in all of my experiences that has given me more pleasure. This was an unsolicited decision that was grace upon grace.

I spent nine of the most gratifying years of my ministry in retirement at Stonebridge United Methodist Church in McKinney. As director of church development, I bought the land on which this church is located. (I am not absolute about this, but my memory seems to validate it.)

Jane and I started going there while the congregation was meeting in a school. When the new sanctuary opened, with the consent of the pastor, I went on staff as a volunteer and served in several capacities for nine years.

While there, I offered the pastoral prayer every Sunday. I later had the prayers placed in a book titled *Prayers for the Pew*. I did signings at all of my former pastorates, as well as the senior residence where I live. The book can still be ordered from Amazon.

I will always be grateful to Stonebridge Church for their hospitality and generosity. To honor one's name is to honor you. No greater honor has ever been bestowed upon me!

CHAPTER 28

Golf: A Minister's Respite

There is an old cliché: "All work and no play makes Jack a dull boy!" Most ministers I know work an inordinate amount of time and are under an inordinate amount of pressure, therefore needing a respite. For me, that respite was golf. I was good enough to enjoy the competition but not good enough to think of being on the PGA Tour. On my best days, I have shot par. On my worst days, I thought about taking up water polo or wrestling alligators.

A respite is a time-out. When the pressures of life begin to close in upon us, we need to be able to open the petcock and let a little steam escape. Life has a way of closing in upon us, and we need to find a way to unwind, relax, and debrief. A respite never puts more pressure upon us; rather, it is something like a soothing massage with a few bumps and bruises.

In one of my appointments, I was superintendent of a given district. The district parsonage was located on the first fairway of a city-owned and operated golf course. My fellow players and I maintained a regular schedule of playing every Thursday, weather permitting. I always looked forward to the great fellowship we enjoyed and to a splendid round of golf, regardless of the score. I have been playing golf for over sixty years and have enjoyed the game immensely. One does not have to score well to enjoy the game, but scoring well enhances the enjoyment.

My regular partner had a way of talking to himself, and when I asked him why he did so, he had a stock answer: "Because I like talking to a smart man, and I like to hear a smart man talk!"

On a particular day, I scheduled a district golf outing and invited anyone and everyone who served in my district. We must have had thirty to thirty-five golfers mulling around the clubhouse waiting for our tee times. I decided to stroll out to the parking lot to see if we had any late arrivals when I noticed one of my district ministers getting out of his car. He was impeccably dressed in dark slacks, a beautifully tailored dress shirt, and freshly shined alligator loafers, heading for the clubhouse. I asked him if he had come to play golf, and he said that he had. I reminded him to retrieve his golf clubs, but he informed me that he did not have any. I foolishly reminded him to put on his golf shoes, but he said he did not have any golf shoes either. Golf balls? No!

I escorted him into the golf shop, rented him a set of clubs, and bought him a few golf balls and a new golf glove. I felt, under the conditions, that was about all I could do for him. He had never before played the game and obviously knew little about the equipment needed for the outing, but he was terrifically excited about being there. I placed him into a foursome and tried to stay as far away from him as I could until the round was over. I am not sure if I ever saw his foursome again, but from that day on he became an avid fan of the game and later the first African-American pastor of Custer Road United Methodist Church.

I have had the good fortune to play some of the top golf courses known to mankind. Along with one of my sons, we played a course in Switzerland where the Swiss Open was played. I cannot remember the name of the course, but I do know that the measurement was laid out in meters instead of yards. I was totally unaware of that, and to my knowledge, I drove over every green (no doubt because of the altitude), to the chagrin of the foursome ahead of us. You would have thought that a man of my knowledge and skill would have figured that out before we finished eighteen holes. I must have had a double portion of Wheaties that morning and later thought how impressive I was at driving the golf ball so far.

I also played Old St. Andrews on a trip to Northern Scotland. I thought someone had posted the wrong yardage on most of the holes, and I spent my quota of strokes trying to blast out of the pot bunkers. My caddy quit before my round was over, but I endured to the end.

I was most fortunate to have been invited to play in two of the Byron Nelson Pro-Ams. I am sure that there could have been many other courses, including the Dallas Country Club, the Dallas National, Stonebridge Ranch and Dye Courses, several courses in the Hawaiian Islands, where the Swiss Open is played, and others of renown.

At my age now, golf is still fun but double the pleasure (if you know what I mean).

Recreation is nothing less or more than 're-creation.' Everyone needs a little diversion in their life.

CHAPTER 29

Honor Flight 25 to Washington, DC, 2015

I was invited to go on Honor Flight 25 from Dallas–Fort Worth to Washington, DC, as a veteran of the Korean War, a two-day event in June 2015. I was required to take someone with me as a companion to look out after my personal needs, and my oldest son, Stephen, was a willing and able assistant.

We flew from DFW on Friday, June 12, and returned on Saturday, June 13, a whirlwind trip in which we visited all of the military and most of the national historic monuments in Washington, DC. Some of the major attractions were the Washington Monument, the Lincoln Memorial, the World War II Memorial, the Korean Memorial, the Air Force Memorial, and the Iwo Jima Memorial, along with a stop at Arlington National Cemetery.

When we visited the Arlington National Cemetery, we went by the tomb of America's most decorated WWII soldier, Audie Murphy. As we approached his place of burial, our guide asked each of us to be prepared to place a quarter on top of his headstone without giving an explanation. After we had followed his request, the guide shared that Audie's nickname had been Two-bits. None of us had ever heard the story.

I experienced a most unique event on the Friday evening we visited the Naval Museum. As we entered the museum, my son and I didn't know exactly where we were to go. We saw a room full of people, and I assumed it was the place assigned for our visit.

After entering the large room, we noticed a naval officer at the front of the room in a receiving line. We quickly assumed that we were in the wrong place and turned to exit the room when an older man approached me. I had on a naval cap with the name of my former ship, the USS *Helena* (CA-75), printed at the top of my cap above the bill. The man looked at me and then at my cap, and he said, "Were you once aboard the USS *Helena*?"

I said that I was. He turned toward the naval officer in the reception line and said, "Don, come here, quick!" Of course, the officer did not come because he was in the receiving line. The man I was talking to was the officer's father. In a very few seconds, the father said to his son, "Don, come right here right now!"

The officer immediately left the receiving line and came to where we were standing. When he arrived, he took one look at my cap and one look at me and said, "Were you aboard the *Helena*?" I responded that I was. Then, to my utter surprise, he said, "I am the retiring commander of the USS *Helena*, which is now a nuclear submarine."

I must say how surprised I was because, when I was aboard the *Helena*, it was a heavy cruiser named after the capital city of Helena, Montana. My ship was cut up into scrap metal in the mid-1960s. Little did I know that the nomenclature after which ships were named had changed sometime long after I was discharged. When I was in the service, one could always determine the type of ship by its name. For example, battleships were named after states, aircraft carriers were named after famous battles, and submarines were named after fish. (The US Department of Defense will do whatever it wants without asking former navy personnel for permission.)

We also visited one of the air force bases in the Washington, DC, area, and when we arrived, several of the top officers of the base were on hand to greet us and to escort us into a large auditorium, where we were greeted and entertained by perhaps the top orchestra related to the air force. Female servicepeople were on hand to dance with the "old veterans." It was quite an evening.

We were then taken to the airport for our return trip home, exhausted from our whirlwind trip. Upon boarding the plane, there was a "mail call" during which each veteran was given a sack of mail from their family and friends back home. I will never forget the letters I received thanking me for my military service. It has been three years since the event, but it has made a permanent impression on my life.

CHAPTER 30

A Return to Korea

I received an invitation, along with other Korean War veterans, to revisit Korea in appreciation for services rendered during the Korean War. It was a gracious invitation, with most of our expenses paid. Our visit required us to bring a companion in case we had developed some debilitating health issues over the fifty-seven years since we had seen duty in and around their country.

I took my daughter, Lori, who proved to be an excellent companion and a much-appreciated helper in my advanced years. (It seems a bit peculiar to use the term *advanced years* because I was in good health, but it had been a long time and I was almost eighty-seven years of age.)

My daughter and I were very excited about going to Korea, a foreign country in Asia that she had never dreamed of visiting, and to have nine days together to revel in our relationship, which was such a blessing. What a marvelous opportunity it was for father and daughter to share such an intimate time together. I cherished the moment and will never forget it.

We flew Korean Airlines from DFW to Seoul in only fourteen hours, but it seemed much longer. My daughter and I were the only two Americans on the flight; all the rest were Koreans. It was a surprise and a delight to have American food served to us on the flight.

When we arrived at the airport, we discovered that it was located in Incheon, on an island offshore from the mainland. The airport is the number-one rated airport in the world. How could we keep from being impressed? We were greeted by an entourage of Korean natives, our first taste of Asian hospitality. On our arrival, we were told that wheelchairs and walkers were available for those who needed assistance. My daughter asked if I would like one of the conveyances, and I told her, "I am walking out of this sucker!" Escalators were everywhere! After what seemed like eternity, we arrived at baggage claim, retrieved our baggage, and headed for the buses.

The Han River separates the "Old Town" from the "New Town." Once we retrieved our luggage, we began our journey through Incheon toward Seoul. I had served two tours in Korea during the war, but I had never set foot on Korean soil.

The Korean people could not have been more cordial. Their appreciation for the American servicemen was far beyond anyone's expectations. On any occasion, when we were invited to a special function, they made us feel as if we were the only people present and that we were very special.

Seoul has a beautiful downtown, with modern transportation and shopping centers. Famous markets are all over the city, where one can purchase quality merchandise at reasonable prices.

Lori and I were housed in a beautiful five-star hotel, the Grand Ambassador. We spent one night there, stored our luggage, and left for Cheorwon for two nights and three days. We headed to the demilitarized zone, or DMZ. (More about that trip later.) This was an exciting moment for all of us. The DMZ rang with intrigue, for we knew nothing about what we were about to experience.

Once there, I saw more coils of razor wire than I had ever seen. Two countries, once united, had been separated for almost seventy years, with little likelihood of ever being reunited. There was a cold, dark uncertain feeling in the air that can haunt one's imagination.

One of the unique things we experienced was a short train ride into one of the tunnels that was approximately six and a half feet high, close to the average height of a North Korean soldier. There were four tunnels altogether that had been dug over a ten-year period by North Korea. At the present, there are no significant uses for the tunnels except grim reminders for what could have been if they had been completed and used for sinister purposes.

We visited one place where a North Korean soldier stood with his back toward the south, and the South Korean soldier stood with his back toward the north. I silently wondered if, while they were standing guard at night and no one could see them, one of them might say to the other, "Hey, brother, do you have a cigarette?" or "Do you have an aspirin on you?" Life is to be shared. How can we treat each other with disdain twenty-four hours a day?

My mind went back over sixty-five years of time and thought how terrible this was—that two brothers were on two sides of barbed wire with no conversation between them all these years, with no hope of ever closing the gap.

The city of Seoul is extremely large as it is home to perhaps 40 percent of the South Korean population, which numbers approximately 55 million. The vast majority are apartment dwellers. Practically everywhere we looked were clusters of apartment complexes, generally three to five buildings sharing a small piece of acreage. The buildings appeared to be twenty-five to thirty stories tall.

Seoul is as modern as any US city, and it is one of the safest cities in the world. Lori and I were not out much at night for the days wore us out, but when we were on the streets, we felt perfectly safe. In fact, I do not remember seeing one police officer. Law enforcement officers can often deter crime simply through their presence, but here was a crimeless city even in their absence.

The veterans group went back to Seoul for the remainder of the trip. What a magnificent city and a gorgeous country! South Korea is the benchmark for what a country can accomplish in a few short years. Its technology is unrivaled. Who has not heard of Samsung or Hyundai?

We were getting ready to close out our trip, and what a trip it had been. I want to leave you with these two great stories.

Story 1

Before we left the United States to go to Korea, we were told to take with us several inexpensive gifts to share with the people of Korea as tokens of our appreciation. Personally, I did not have any idea of what I would take with me that might pique the interest of the people of Korea. After much thought, though, I decided to rob my lockbox and take a package of two-dollar bills. I had been collecting them for several years.

After we arrived, I made selective choices as to whom would receive my gifts. One was the bus driver who transported us to various points of interest. When I presented him with a two-dollar bill, the driver looked at it, turned it over, and looked at it from every side, making odd sounds. He looked at me as if to ask, "Is this real? Is this American currency?"

I shared with him that it was quite rare but was actual currency. As I presented several of these gifts, each was received with deep appreciation.

On the last afternoon of our trip, before the honor ceremony that evening, the bus driver took us to one of the great museums in the city. As we were concluding our tour, my daughter said to me, "Dad, why don't you present one of the souvenirs I brought to one of the little girls huddled within the hallway of the museum?" There must have been six or seven little girls dressed in what I assumed were uniforms representing some youth organization in which they participated.

I walked over to the huddle and tapped on the shoulder of the smallest one in the group. When she turned around, her eyes struck me at about waist level. With heightened interest, she lifted her head upward until our eyes met, and great surprise registered on her face.

I said to her, "I have brought to you a gift from America in appreciation for your wonderful hospitality." I handed her one of the gifts my daughter had brought, which I had not seen.

The gift was in a sack. She took the sack, removed the gift, and looked at it with great interest. She turned the gift around and looked at it from every angle. It was a sports pennant. After looking at it for several seconds, a gleam came to her eye and a smile formed on her face. She exclaimed in a high-pitched voice, "Ohh! *Ohh!* The Dallas Cowboys! They are my dad's favorite team!" With that she leaped up and hugged my neck.

As my daughter and I were walking away, I heard the patter of small feet. I looked back, and here she came! She jumped up and gave me another hug, and away she went. I have thought time and time again, *How many little girls in Korea would even know who the Dallas Cowboys are?* Incidentally, I did send this story to the owner of the Dallas Cowboys but unfortunately have never heard from him.

Closing Banquet

The last night I spent in Korea was one of the greatest moments of my life. It was a night of the unexpected. Never have I been so surprised or so honored!

We veterans had been on a tour of the city most of the day, and we were told to be in the grand ballroom at 5:30 p.m. with coat and tie. I left my room at about a quarter after five, appropriately dressed. When my daughter and I got to the steps going up into the ballroom, I noticed men on either end of each step clapping enthusiastically for our arrival. We made a short left turn to another set of stairs leading up into the ballroom with men on each step, again applauding. Tears flowed.

Once we were in the ballroom, we were given our table numbers and escorted to our tables. To my utter surprise, I was being seated at the head table. My daughter, though, was seated at another table. In a few minutes, an army general of some rank was seated to my right, and his wife was seated at his right. I made a cursory glance at his shoulder and saw bright, shiny stars on each epaulet.

After acquiring the courage, I said, "General, may I have the permission to ask you what your assignment is?" He graciously responded with words that untied my shoes. (I cannot reveal his name, rank, or duty assignment due to classified information.) Never have I been so honored.

As the grand finale to the evening, each of the nineteen veterans was honored with a ribbon placed around his neck, at the end of which was a shiny gold peace medal referred to as the Ambassador Peace Medal.

The next day, we flew back to the States filled with memories that will last forever.

During the first week of December 2006, Jane and I moved from McKinney, Texas, where we had lived for sixteen years, to Highland Springs, a newly opened, private, total-care facility built on eighty-nine acres of land formerly owned by Texas A&M Agricultural Extension Farm on Frankford Road at Coit.

Highland Springs is a senior (buy-in) facility that offers numerous services and upscale living conditions. We own our own two-bedroom, two-bath condominium with a living room and dining Room overlooking a large pond, manicured grounds, and beautiful trees, complete with adequate parking for everyday usage.

Each apartment comes with a kitchen furnished with all the appliances and cabinets. A laundry room with appliances is also installed and maintained.

Each unit is air-conditioned, and utilities, taxes, and insurance provided, except for owners' belongings. Highland Springs has a twenty-four-hour security staff available in case of medical emergency. We have a fully staffed medical center with four physicians plus a podiatrist, plus an auxiliary wing that has other medical specialists who come in for scheduled appointments.

Highland Springs also has a first-class transportation department that supplies most every need. We have an indoor, heated pool with a hot tub, as well as scheduled exercise classes most weekdays. There is a well-designed and functioning fitness center and a computer room with a printer. In addition, a bank, post office, green house, garden plots, extended care center (five-star), and many other opportunities—far too many to name—are nearby.

The dining services equal the facilities. Dinner is served in the Chisholm Restaurant, and lighter fare is available in the grill. There is another restaurant in Pecan Grove, with a third one to be opened in the future.

Highland Springs often offers regular entertainment of different genres. Various speakers present programs on topics ranging from political to religious and everything in between. If Highland Springs doesn't have it, either it is not available or you do not need it.

We are a true community, a large, friendly family of the retired, and we are ready and willing to serve and be served. It is my home!

CHAPTER 31

Defining the Work of a District Superintendent

Be prepared for the unexpected.

The work of the superintendent is demanding. The office is an extension of the bishop's office in an administrative capacity, serving as an arm of his office in a particular geographic territory. There is a very close working relationship between the bishop and each superintendent. The superintendent has certain liberties but needs to have access to the bishop at all times. Hardly a day goes by—and never a week—that the superintendent doesn't need to visit or confer with the bishop on matters of mutual interest.

The district superintendent is, in corporate language, the executive officer of every church under his or her supervision, as well as all of the auxiliary ministries within the confines of the district. From day to day, certain misunderstandings tend to separate rather than unite. All are free to conduct the affairs of their offices within certain limits of their responsibilities. If conflict arises, honest dialogue should take place between the parties involved. There should be a level of trust within the arena of our particular responsibilities, but there should never be a time when dialogue becomes impossible. It may be necessary to invite a third party to any meeting where disharmony prevails in order to ensure that the rights of all parties are respected and given due process.

Superintendents need to visit each of the churches on certain occasions. The three most obvious are 1) to visit the pastor concerning his or her appointment status and to discuss how the appointment is functioning and whether or not an appointment is stable; 2) to visit with the pastor-parish committee with the same agenda (one of the occasional problems that arises is that the pastor is the chairperson of the nominating committee and may have the influence to seed the committee with too many supporters; this is not always a problem, but there are exceptions); 3) to preside over the annual charge/church conference to objectively evaluate the year's accomplishments with the elected personnel. It can be a most productive meeting in that it builds momentum for the upcoming year.

The time required to do the job means that superintendents are away from their families from September through December, placing quite a strain upon superintendents and their families. I understand that charge conferences have been conducted in cluster settings in recent days. The question I raise is how effective they are. The approach of giving individual attention is still more appealing to me, but how can I knock it since I haven't tried it? The other question is, how can a local church get the proper attention and affirmation in cluster settings?

All Cases Handled Judiciously

Where there are some critical issues concerning work habits or obvious inabilities to perform effectively in certain areas or certain suspicious or proven indiscretions, it becomes the responsibility of the superintendent to bring matter to light and deal with them in a judicious manner. When the bishop needs to be informed, it should be done with integrity and full knowledge of all persons concerned.

When a pastor commits an act contrary to the discipline and the superintendent is forced to meet with the congregation concerning the violation, who is directly on the spot? Often, it is the superintendent! There should never be a me-versus-them situation. A disciplinary violation is just that; it is not a personal grudge on either side of the argument. It is an act in response to a law that has been violated, and it should never become personal.

When a pastor or superintendent is accused of an act contrary to the discipline, some action is required. The superintendent or bishop must be prepared to assume responsibility to take appropriate action without regard to retaliation. If the discipline is the law of the church, let us be prepared to follow the law.

CHAPTER 32

Theological Principles for Spiritual Growth

John Wesley, founder of the Methodist movement in England, as part of his heritage, developed guidelines for our spiritual development. Wesley had a unique way of understanding and explaining the doctrine of grace. Grace covers the whole of a person's life in three different perspectives. It is a matter of interpreting which phase we are experiencing at any given time.

What I intend to do through this chapter is to allow the reader to identify with me as I experience and move from one phase to another, growing more deeply spiritual in each phase and expressing my faith more maturely as I move through my ministry.

Wesley understood grace as being acknowledged and expressed in three different ways. He called the first phase prevenient grace. By this he meant that the divine love of God surrounds all humanity and precedes any and all of our conscious impulses and actions. God takes the initiative to pursue a relationship with us and urges us to turn toward Him so that we may be cleansed from our bondage of sin and death. Since it is our original nature to assume that we are able to solve our own issues, God must break through to us.

We need to understand that God silently intervenes in our lives, and it is the Spirit in us that we must discover as we decide for ourselves the direction in which we will go. This begins a primitive movement that must be recognized and followed. People have the opportunity to pursue and create a climate between themselves and God that enables God to work His way in their lives that produces the desired relationship.

The second phase Wesley refers to is justifying grace. Anyone who relies on the law is under a curse. When we live under grace, we live under a different mandate: "The one who is righteous will live by faith." It must become our responsibility to know the difference between law and grace, and it must be our personal responsibility to choose grace above law. As we mature beyond prevenient grace, we understand that we take on more and more through free will to follow God more sincerely and completely.

The third phase Wesley calls sanctifying grace. God continues to nurture our growth in grace as a continual journey toward "having the mind of Christ and walking as He walked." "Do you expect to be made perfect in this life?" is a question the bishop asks every ministerial candidate wishing to be ordained. When I stood before the bishop to answer his question, I thought, *If I answer no, he may not ordain me. If I answer yes, I run the risk of lying.* I wasn't sure I could answer it truthfully because I knew something of the person within who wasn't perfect. It was a spiritual dilemma. Yet I thought I would reword the phrase to "Do you promise to live your life as a child of God, growing slowly in His Spirit, hoping to be made as perfect as God can make you?" I am sure I answered the question to the bishop's satisfaction because I was ordained in 1965 at the age of thirty-five years. I am now eighty-seven and still serving the Lord, perhaps with less energy but with spirit that honors His name.

CHAPTER 33

Pastors Are Eligible for Continuing Education

Some of the greatest opportunities I have had have involved domestic and foreign travel. Few things can enable a pastor to be more widely recognized and informative than traveling and experiencing the beautiful and culturally diverse world God has created. Travel is one of the highest forms of continuing education.

During my many years in ministry, I have had the opportunity to travel to at least thirty countries, as well as to all fifty states. Much of my travel has been arranged by tour companies that specialize in continuing education for the clergy and congregation members. Multiple tour companies offer pastors special gratuitous privileges if they can recruit a particular number of travelers to accompany the pastor on a given tour. I mention a few in particular that I have thoroughly enjoyed.

Wesley Heritage Tour to England

This is of particular interest to people with Methodist roots. The tour visits a number of locations relating to the founder of what became the Methodist Church. History is exciting and educational.

What greater experience is there than to spend ten days to two weeks with laypersons from your parish visiting the roots of our faith tradition?

Our story actually began with the Reverend and Mrs. Samuel Wesley, rector of a small congregation in Epworth, England. The Reverend and Mrs. Wesley had nineteen children, ten of whom survived infancy, among which were John (born 1703) and Charles (three or four years younger than his brother). They were the principal founders of the new church movement known as Methodism. The name was derived from a practice developed by a group of students at Oxford University who, early in the day, would read the scriptures for an hour, pray for an hour, eat breakfast, attend classes, and then visit the orphanages and jails each day. Engaged in this practice, they acquired the name of Methodists because of their rigorous methods. The group liked the name, adopted it, and wove it into the actual name.

The movement spread across England, and ultimately to America, and the name *Methodist* was ultimately adopted as the name of the new movement. The parsonage for the Reverend Samuel Wesley was in Epworth, England, and was set afire by the parishioners—in a strange incident—when John was four years of age. John was trapped in a room on the second floor, but his life was saved by a group of men who formed a human ladder to rescue him. He became known as the child plucked from the burning. His good fortune was seen as an act of God. John became a priest of the Church of England but founded a new movement that crossed the Atlantic and became the Methodist Church in 1784.

Methodism grew up through the 1950s, 1960s, and 1970s to become the largest Protestant denomination in America. It no longer holds that distinction, but it is still a dynamic body of Christians who hold true to Wesley's doctrine of grace.

The church still exists today, set up under an episcopal order with a representative government, numbering in the millions around the world.

Protestant Heritage Tour to Europe

This is an extremely interesting and informative tour that takes visitors to Germany and Switzerland, in particular, with various stops related to the Protestant Reformation. To me, the more interesting people involved are Martin Luther and John Calvin. The Reformation was a revolt against the Roman Catholic Church over the selling of indulgences and other issues Luther found to be contrary to his understanding of the Bible and church practices. Luther was the priest of the church in Wittenberg, Germany. He drew up his grievances and nailed them to the door of the village church on October 31, 1517. Word of his action spread throughout Europe and beyond, bringing a fracture to the Roman Catholic Church and creating a new body referred to as Protestants.

The other figure of Luther's day was a brilliant theologian by the name of John Calvin, a Frenchman who made his teaching headquarters in Geneva, Switzerland. Calvin became the author of a new teaching known as predestination. Many, including Luther, took issue with Calvin over this doctrine. The basic conflict was between predestination and free will. The arguments over these doctrines have not been settled for over five hundred years and are not likely to be so in years to come. Denominations have become grouped both for and against them. Other doctrines also theologically divide churches but, in my opinion, none more seriously than these two.

Within a few short years, the fracture jumped the English Channel to England proper, and the king of England, Henry VIII, split with the Roman Church and founded the Church of England, or what we know as the Anglican tradition. This break gave the Protestants a foothold outside of Europe proper and set the stage for a significant migration to the Western world. New forms of church organizations came into being with the settlement of the Colonies in the eastern part of the United States, destined to move westward as the population shifted to unsettled territories.

When I came into ministry in the middle 1950s, there were

basically three hundred different denominations in America, mostly from Protestant beginnings. Today, religious sociologists say that the number of different religious groupings may total as many as two thousand.

But the expansion of denominationalism has created a desire in the adherents to examine their historic roots, which has them traveling back to the continent of Europe, creating a boon for the travel industry.

The Nation of Israel

Perhaps there is no country in the world that enjoys greater tourism than Israel. The history of the Israelites in the Old Testament, according to many scholars, covers a period beginning approximately with Abraham in around 1750 BC until the exile into Babylon in 587 BC. If this is true, there was no Israel until the rebirth of the nation in AD 1948 orchestrated by Great Britain.

I was very fortunate to be able to lead a group of church members to the Holy Land on a trip organized about five years ago through Educational Opportunities, located in Lakeland Florida. Educational Opportunities is a wonderful company that handles most of the trips from the United States to Israel.

We traveled approximately the length of the country from the southern border to northern Galilee, visiting many of the sites believed to be authentic. There is such a known history due to the readership, but the world's oldest cultures cannot compare to Israel.

What I found to be the most inconsistent with religious literature is the conflict between the Israelites and the Palestinians. There are more fences and walls between Palestine and Israel than there are between the Republicans and the Democrats in Washington, DC. Indeed, Washington, DC, is a walled city.

The attraction of traveling to Israel is to relive the days of old when the people were in search of the Messiah. What a rich tradition Israel has in the concept of the prophecy concerning the coming of the Messiah. It is a prophecy that goes back centuries and that speaks a great deal about a future filled with promises of love and hope and all the things humankind needs to live together in perfect harmony only to witness the discord of modern civilization. One is not lifted to levels of hope and peace; rather, one is left in total despair of there ever being a lasting peace in the land of brotherly love.

I live in a community where love abounds among the races, classes, and religious groupings. Why look for something I already have? We cannot give up looking for something that promises more and fulfills more. But the mandate of humanity is to live where you are and make of it the kingdom of God.

Printed in the United States
By Bookmasters